How to Worship in Spirit and Truth

JERRY ZIRKLE

WORD & SPIRIT
PUBLISHING

How to Worship in Spirit and Truth
ISBN: 978-1949106-83-1

Published by Word and Spirit Publishing
P.O. Box 701403
Tulsa, Oklahoma 74170
wordandspiritpublishing.com

Acknowledgments

David Ingles, my lifelong friend, and brother in Christ, changed my life through his anointing and gift to pen new-creation songs like none other for the Body of Christ. His friendship, creativity, and love made this book possible. His music was the new song the Holy Spirit had told me to sing years ago. Without his music, many of the stories, experiences, and miracles in this book might never have happened.

The contributing writer and editor who oversaw this entire project from start to finish is my faithful friend, Jan Fields. The Holy Spirit told me I would author books from my supernatural experiences with Him over thirty years ago. I am beyond thankful for Jan's commitment and willingness to support me in this process.

Keith Provance and his team at Word and Spirit Publishing are new friends and collaborators on this book. Upon our first contact, I knew he understood spiritual realities and that he was God's choice for this project. I am so thankful for his heart to serve and his years of publishing expertise to facilitate my first book.

Dedication

First, I dedicate this book to our church family, partners, and friends who make Jerry Zirkle Ministries possible. I cannot measure the love, prayer, and financial support you have given into my life and ministry.

Second, family is the most important thing to me, aside from my relationship with my heavenly Father. My wife, Linda, has seen me through the best and worst days, always supporting and loving me through every single step. My five children and their spouses, each of whom I love uniquely, and my fourteen grandchildren—to each member of my family, I dedicate this book.

Contents

Foreword

BROTHER JERRY ZIRKLE AND I ARE "JESUS FRIENDS." OUR first contact was through a recording that Jerry had been given on which I sang and shared. After that, we became friends. Since that time, the Lord has blessed us to minister together numerous times. The following Scriptures help me to describe the anointed ministry of Brother Jerry:

> *Then Samuel took the horn of oil, and anointed him in the midst of his brethren: and the Spirit of the LORD came upon David from that day forward.*
>
> —1 SAMUEL 16:13 KJV

> *And Saul said unto his servants, provide me now a man that can play well, and bring him to me.*
>
> —1 SAMUEL 16:17 KJV

> *Then answered one of the servants, and said, Behold, I have seen a son of Jesse the Bethlehemite, that is cunning in playing, and a mighty valiant man, and*

a man of war, and prudent in matters, and a comely person, and the LORD is with him.

—1 SAMUEL 16:18 KJV

But now bring me a minstrel. And it came to pass, when the minstrel played, that the hand of the LORD came upon him.

—2 KINGS 3:15 KJV

A minstrel is someone who values the Scriptures and is obedient to express them in an exhortative or worshipful manner. People who sing in the church do so as worshipers (of God), but some are minstrels who lead others into worship (with music).

A minstrel can be a musical performer in or out of a spiritual gathering. They are loyal, positive, patient, flexible, caring, and humble (as a harpist, guitarist, pianist, or organist). They can also be a singer of verses or melodies to the accompaniment of a harp or other musical instrument.

As a Christian troubadour, Brother Jerry shares and sings psalms to the Lord while people worship in God's presence. Anointed songs defeat the enemy, advance deliverance, stretch boundaries, and encourage families!

Both Jerry and I harmoniously proclaim: "THY STATUTES HAVE BEEN MY SONGS IN THE HOUSE OF MY PILGRIMAGE" (Psalm 119:54).

—DAVID INGLES

Preface

To every thing there is a season, and a time to every purpose under the heaven.

—ECCLESIASTES 3:1 KJV

WHEN I FIRST STARTED IN THE TRAVELING MINISTRY AFTER graduating from Rhema Bible Training Center in 1981, God told me one of the last things I would do in this life was to put into print what He and I have done together. In due time, I would share the revelation that Holy Spirit taught me from the Word of God and the faith adventures we would have together.

One of the biblical truths in which God profoundly used me was spiritual worship. As a radio broadcaster for over seventy years and a traveling psalmist/prophetic minister, Holy Spirit trained me to hear His voice and to operate in the supernatural. As a pastor and teacher, I taught and demonstrated by precept and example how to minister in Spirit and in truth. The inevitable result is that we witnessed God move mightily in our church.

This book is primarily composed of my teachings during a weeklong *Psalminar* on the campus of Oral Roberts University, where my longtime friend David Ingles and I taught together. The purpose of this *Psalminar* was to teach biblical truths, to worship God, and to bring a demonstration of the Spirit into our services. As a psalmist, I taught spiritual and practical insights from my pastoral and ministerial experiences while functioning in the various fivefold offices. This book is a compilation of those principles, along with nuggets of truth and practical ministry guidelines gleaned from a lifetime of ministry.

My heart is that the life of God exudes from the pages of this book and sparks an inextinguishable fire in the spirits of ministers, students, and everyday believers. May the Holy Ghost use it to answer questions regarding the local church, how to lead worship, the ministry of helps, following the call of God, the traveling ministry, and much more.

I also want this book to help restore a higher level of spiritual worship to the Body of Christ, so that we all move into greater manifestations of the Holy Ghost. My prayer is that the book's principles open the eyes of ministers to biblical patterns of spiritual worship (as described by both Jesus and the apostle Paul) in the New Testament. And my hope is that these truths help to school individual believers into faith and power through music that transforms our minds until we all talk like, walk like, and act like Jesus in the earth.

As we move into more accurate and purer New Testament worship, may we experience greater degrees of the miraculous in this Holy Ghost dispensation before the second coming of Jesus. To God be the Glory!

Introduction

Blessed are they which do hunger and thirst after righteousness.

—MATTHEW 5:6 KJV

AS A FOLLOWER OF CHRIST SINCE I WAS A YOUNG BOY, I HAVE served God my entire life. But there was one specific season in which I became hungry for God as never before. This hunger caused the Spirit of God to bring me into a deeper life with Christ. In my quest to know more of God, I began to learn about God's fullness and how victory and success were available to me in this life. Before that, I had loved Jesus, but I did not know about the authority and power God had made available to every believer through Christ.

The greatest change in my Christian life came when God revealed who *I* was in Christ and the authority He had given to *me*. Learning about my authority in Christ and the power I had as a new creation (through my words and music) directed me to a new adventure with God.

This new frontier set me on a path that would change everything. As a result of this fresh manna from heaven, my walk in the Spirit opened the door to signs and wonders as I followed the Spirit's direction. In so many instances, I boldly did what the Holy Spirit spoke even when my mind was telling me it was a bad idea. The results were miraculous, time after time. Learning to follow the hidden man of the heart led me to unstoppable victory.

It is a powerful thing what God did in *redemption* through Christ. The word redemption means "to buy back." In Colossians 1:13, the Bible tells us that we were translated (redeemed) out of the hand of Satan's kingdom and into the Kingdom of God's Son, and that this was secured for us at the new birth. However, salvation is only the beginning of this new life in Christ. Just as God created His universe with words, as His new creations, made in His image, we change our universe, our world, and our atmosphere with our words. Without a change in our words, our life still reflects one who is defeated, sick, and miserable—that is, the man before Christ.

I challenge you to propel yourself to a greater and fuller capacity in your service to God. Remember, Holy Spirit is always calling us to a higher level, and there are no limits with God. May I compel you to press into the call of God, as the apostle Paul admonishes us in Philippians 3:14: "press toward the mark for the prize of the high calling of God in Christ Jesus" (KJV). May this be your daily confession as you commit to all God has planned for you in this generation.

This is our finest hour!

Chapter One

My Life of Music and Miracles

I chose you before I formed you in the womb; I set you apart before you were born. I appointed you a prophet to the nations.

—JEREMIAH 1:5 KJV

A VISION OF MY FUTURE AND GOD'S PURPOSE AND PLANS for me unfolded in my childhood, similar to what happened to Jeremiah: "Before you saw the light of day, I had holy plans for you" (Jer. 1:5 MSG). I was born and raised in Akron, Ohio, with a strong godly matriarch. Mom took her eight kids to the Cottage Grove Evangelical Church, where she served as a charter member. As a result, church became an integral part of our family life.

My dad, on the other hand, developed and built luxury homes for people as a business owner. He taught me many godly principles of integrity and moral character, even though he was not a Christian. My dad found Christ later in his life while he was fighting cancer. With a strong moral and Christian foundation, I grasped many lessons in our home, family business, and local church. These foundational principles of God became a launching pad into Christian ministry for me.

Coming from a musical family, I learned to play the guitar at a very young age. I also learned to play a cello, steel guitar, mandolin, violin, and all stringed instruments, and I could pick out keys on a piano when composing music. As a young boy, I began writing music, not realizing these musical and poetic talents were gifts from God. I thought everyone could write a poem extemporaneously or off-the-cuff, as I could. There was not a life event that I could not pen lyrics and a tune about, describing people's life experiences. Little did I know this was the psalmist ministry God would develop in my life.

My brother Bob, who is six years older than me, introduced me to Rev. P.L. Wiseman, the pastor of the Winter

Green Ledges Church of God in Akron, Ohio. Pastor Wiseman invited Bob and me to join him as traveling ministers when he went out on revivals or evangelistic meetings.

Pastor Wiseman became a real mentor and friend. He invested much energy, time, and spiritual knowledge into us. Bob and I were his music team for the radio program he sponsored in Akron, Ohio, on the WADC radio station. I remember those early days as a small boy, playing and singing on the radio with Bob. We also attended Pastor Wiseman's church on Sunday evenings and provided music for his services.

I am indebted both to the Church of God and to the Evangelical church for providing a strong foundational groundwork and understanding of church government and its operation. Having this hands-on training prepared and equipped me for the pastoral ministry to which God would call me. Along with the Winter Green Church of God influence, the other strong spiritual impact on my life was the Cottage Grove Evangelical Church, where I grew up. This, too, became a place of great growth and development. I learned all facets of ministry through my involvement in the music ministry, as a Bible teacher, church trustee, steward, and church delegate at conferences.

Those first years of ministry with both churches provided ministry experiences that gave me a greater understanding of pastoring as well as field ministry. These churches provided so much natural understanding of the working of a church organization, and many unique facets of ministry became established in my thinking during those days.

Growing up playing music, ministering on the radio, and serving in our Evangelical church was a way of life. The radio ministry opened many doors for me as I ministered in churches throughout Ohio, West Virginia, Michigan, Kentucky, Indiana, and Pennsylvania. Little did I know the marvelous networking tool that radio would become in my life and ministry.

As I followed the open doors, the favor of God, and the leading of the Holy Spirit, the path of radio always seemed to be the guiding light of my ministry, both then and now. It was not until much later that I understood the leading of the Spirit from Scripture. In looking back, I surely see the hand of God directing my steps and taking me from one place of ministry to another.

After meeting Linda, my wife, and getting married, I continued to travel until Linda Lou, my first child, was born. She was the joy and rejoicing of our hearts. God dealt with me to establish roots and raise my family. I knew in my heart that putting my family first was now the priority of my life. During the next twelve years, my wife and I had five children, who made our lives so fulfilled, meaningful, and busy. All the while, we were still very involved in the Cottage Grove Evangelical Church, and I continued doing radio. After twenty-plus years of traveling with Bob, I finally stopped the ministry team on the road, but we continued the radio ministry.

In the seventies, the charismatic move of the Holy Spirit gained momentum in churches around the United States, and even globally. It spurred a great desire for more of God in the denominational churches. Due to many pastors' reluctance to acknowledge and move with the Holy Ghost, these charismatic preachers began to teach on neutral ground. Men began to teach on bodily healing and living by faith, which Jesus preached and demonstrated during the first century. People started learning that God was not mad at them, but that He had sent His Son as an atonement for both sin and sickness for every man, woman, boy, and girl. This fresh manna from the Word of God brought signs and wonders into these meetings and into the lives of the people of God.

My introduction to this move of God was a result of the intercessors in our church witnessing my hunger for God. They started sharing "faith" and "Holy Ghost" books with me. The first book on faith I read was by Kenneth E. Hagin called *Authority of the Believer.*[1] A hunger for God like never before came over me as I read that book. The more I read and studied these faith books, the hungrier I got. I realized God had so much more for the believer than I knew anything about.

During this time, I taught a college-age and young couples' class. It began as a small nucleus of people and grew to over two hundred young people meeting every week to study the subject of faith. It filled a great void of hunger for truth in their lives. In this college-age class, I instructed them using Brother Kenneth Hagin's book *New Thresholds of Faith*.[2] It was meaty, so it took quite a while to get through the book. The people in this class began to spiritually grow from the study of the Word of God.

One Easter Sunday in the late seventies, while I was teaching this Bible class, an unwed mother brought her new baby to my class. The baby had been born with club feet. That day I was teaching on Philippians 3:10, "That I may know him, and the power of his resurrection" (KJV). As she heard this message about the power of God to heal, she said, "If that is true, then God will heal my baby." Before I had time to say anything, she stuck her baby's feet into my hands. Instantly the baby's feet began to snap, crackle, and pop like Rice Krispies, and immediately they were made whole—all to my shock and amazement.

This miracle caused a great stir in the church. By the time the morning church service began, news of this baby's miracle reached the pastor. He preached that morning on how miracles were not for today. He told the congregation how his mother had died a horrible death. He lashed out at healing and praying in tongues. I was the only one in the church teaching healing. However, I never taught anyone about speaking in tongues in the church. He threw that in for good measure.

The pastor told me, "If you pray in those other tongues, we don't even want you on our parking lot." I had put that parking lot in almost singlehandedly myself. I had been on the pulpit committee and even helped to approve this new pastor to our church, but I received the "left foot of fellowship" that day from this Evangelical church that my mom had helped start. I had given many years of hard work and labor in this church, but it was my promotion day. God had so much more in store for me.

A Journey of Faith

I was so hungry for God that after the excommunication from my church, I went to the streets and began ministering to the hippies. They were getting born again, filled with the Holy Ghost, and prophesying. I did not know anything about the gifts of the Spirit at that time. It was among these hippies that I first saw the gifts of the Spirit manifest. In fact, a leader called out a word of knowledge for a hernia in the first service I attended, and God healed me on the spot. After seeing the gifts of the Spirit manifest, I was never the same again!

We read Jesus' words in the gospel of Matthew: "Hunger and thirst for righteousness, and they will be filled" (Matt. 5:6 niv). I wanted to do something for God. I knew the value of radio since I had been on radio for years by this time. I prayed, *God, if I can find a man who will preach the Gospel, not gripe at people, not ride people's cases, but just preach the Word and preach the message of faith around the world, I would sell everything I have to get him into Akron.* I believed in the laws of sowing and reaping and the principle of harvest long before I understood it clearly from the Word of God. I thought, *If I cashed in everything I owned, it would probably bring in enough money to start teaching the word of faith on the radio.*

At that time, being on the radio was expensive. I knew if I could get down to the bare necessities and live a little cheaper, I could buy more radio time. My plan was to buy more radio time for a preacher teaching the word of faith in my city. If I had to buy it on three or four stations, I was going to do it. Now, that may sound crazy to you. *But it was so alive in me!*

I started out on this new journey in God with the dream, passion, and purpose in my heart to get out of debt. My desire to get out of debt was not to pay bills, or even to obtain a surplus of money in my pocket. My purpose was so that I could propagate the Gospel.

In 1977, I was working on a salary and always looking for a bargain. I knew I could live cheaper if I could just live plainer and simpler. I could live at a lower level, and we would get the Full Gospel message started in Akron. I knew if I could get the Word started, I would not have to live meagerly and barely get by for very long. I understood that through the law of sowing and reaping, God would bless me. For a while, I got into works because of my insatiable desire to follow God and get out of debt quickly. My motives became a little cloudy.

There is a fine line between acting in faith and mentally assenting to the Word of God. Both faith and mental assent agree to the facts of the Word. However, faith fearlessly acts and does the Word without sense knowledge or physical evidence. On the other hand, mental assent refuses to act on the Word of God. The apostle James said in James 2:17, "Even so faith, if it hath not works, is dead, being alone" (KJV). In the back of my mind, I knew it would not take long until God would restore me. This great sacrifice of tightening my belt to obtain financing to fund a faith preacher to proclaim the Full Gospel on the radio in Akron was temporary.

I knew God had called me to preach for a lifetime. I did not commit to preach for a season, waiting until all the conditions were perfect. My call was a total surrender to God for the long haul. In preparation to get out of debt, I cut up my credit cards. God did not bail me out, nor did He deliver me immediately. Instead, I went through two of the most agonizing years of my life. My Word level was insufficient to sustain my giving efforts. My understanding and my grasp of the word of faith was not enough to sustain me while I was working a job.

I quit my job because it was not enough to accomplish my vision of bringing a faith preacher to Akron. I needed more money. So, I quit my job and became a free agent to do whatever I could put my hand to do. I did not realize I had become a wet-water-walker in faith, instead of a dry-boat-rider in my comfort zone. I had gotten out of the boat to walk on the water, just like Peter did that day on the Sea of Galilee with Jesus.

God did redeem and restore me; however, it was not without faith, diligence, and perseverance on my part. There is always God's part and man's part in every journey of faith. God did His part, and I did mine. In fact, I made more money as an entrepreneur than I did working for a company. Finally, I was out of debt.

With this new freedom from debt, one morning my wife, Linda, and I were sitting down at a restaurant. She started making a list of everyone she wanted to bless with money now that we were out of debt. It was not until I got out of debt that God spoke to me and said, *Jerry, now you go learn how to be that man that you are trying to bring into this town.*

Traveling to the Promised Land

Around this time, I discovered Brother Kenneth E. Hagin had a Bible school just outside of Tulsa, Oklahoma. I decided to check out his ministry in person by attending his annual Faith Camp Meeting in Broken Arrow, Oklahoma, in July 1978. In this meeting, I learned how the power of God and faith had changed this man's life, taking him from a deathbed experience to a Gospel ministry filled with signs and wonders.

I learned about the faith of Jesus and how He and other men from the Bible all used faith to receive deliverance and healing, to raise the dead, and to participate in miraculous experiences. Most importantly, I learned God expects believers to live by that same faith. I, too, became a candidate for this kind of faith.

I made the ultimate decision to leave Ohio, head toward the Promised Land, and go to Bible school in my forties. Calling my wife from the camp meeting in Broken Arrow, Oklahoma, I told her we were moving to Oklahoma. I told her to sell or give away everything we had. My wife and I had experienced a lot of blood, sweat, and tears building our home in Ohio, and now we were leaving it behind us. It took as much faith for Linda as it did for me to leave all of it behind! This required us to leave our family, friends, and everything we had established in Ohio, to follow God. We leased our house to a family in Ohio, rented a U-Haul, brought the washer and dryer and the girls' dresses, and left for Bible school.

Church people always told me, "Sell out completely to God." Yet when I decided to follow God and do what the church said was the ultimate sacrifice, it was a far different story. Now they said I was crazy, too old, and I had too many kids to follow God in this way! However, I did receive one encouraging word from an inebriated alcoholic; he said, "Jerry, you cannot leave everything behind without God blessing you." Nonetheless, I knew the call of God on my life, and I risked everything to follow Him. Throughout the following years of ministry, I never regretted the life God gave me for the life I gave up.

In August 1978, I left Ohio and traveled to Broken Arrow, Oklahoma, to attend Rhema Bible Training Center. My younger brother Jim preceded me in coming to Rhema by one year, in the fall of 1977. After Jim graduated from Rhema, he moved to Guatemala, Central America, to pursue mission work and establish a Bible school. This mission is still flourishing today.

Selling my belongings and leaving Ohio was only the tip of the iceberg of the faith that would be required. Learning to overcome in every arena of life and trust in God became not just a journey, but the very essence of my life. I learned hundreds of faith lessons by applying the Word in my life. If you think it is unnerving to live by faith when you are single, add six other dependents to the mix. The challenging opportunities for us were innumerable. God taught me that active, creative faith would put me constantly on the edge of disaster. Only dying to self and pressing into the vision would deliver me out of the disaster that active, creative faith brings.

As I attended Rhema, my personal experiences of faith and trusting God to care for my family and pay for Bible school caused my faith to be the tool to obtain everything I needed. The Bible exhorts us to "walk by faith, not by sight" (2 Cor. 5:7 KJV). In Hebrews 11:6, we learn that "it is impossible to please God without faith." Once the light came regarding the mandate of God to obtain blessings by trusting Him and receiving them by faith, an exciting new life and adventure began.

My faith exploits while at Bible school and raising a family by the Word of God is another story. The stories from that era of walking and living by faith are tales of a lifetime with five teenage girls and boys. In those days, our family went from one miracle to the next, all because of the trust I learned from the Word of God and the necessity to trust God once I had surrendered all other sources to Him. Thank God for Holy Ghost!

Once I graduated from Rhema Bible Training Center, I ventured out on a mission trip to Guatemala, where my brother had started his mission work. I wanted to do something for God. I knew I did not have the call to full-time missions as Jim did, but I wanted to hear what the Holy Ghost might have for me in the mission.

While I was in Guatemala, God spoke to me for eight days and nights about my ministry. He said my place in ministry was not in Guatemala. He told me to return to America as a psalmist, and that He was giving me a new song to sing. The new songs Holy Ghost wanted me to sing were new-creation and redemptive realities. During the time I spent with God in Guatemala, Holy Ghost spoke to me about so many things. He said that He was going to use and place me in front of many people. He was going to place me in the forefront (psalmist) ministry, and then in the fivefold ministry. God has been so faithful to fulfill His Word to me. I have stood before thousands of people over the years, and I have ministered over the radio for decades. The key to miracles is speaking and singing faith that is based in God's Word. For years Oral Roberts told audiences all over the world to *Expect a Miracle!* Expectation is the breeding ground for miracles. The Word of God in music creates an expectation from God. For me, this music of faith and new-creation realities became a way of life and the gateway to miracles. Hallelujah! What a Savior!

Chapter Two

A Psalmist's Ministry

David . . . the anointed of the God of Jacob, and the sweet psalmist of Israel, said,

The Spirit of the LORD spake by me, and his word was in my tongue.

—2 SAMUEL 23:1–2 KJV

THERE IS SO MUCH MISUNDERSTANDING OVER THE ROLE of the psalmist in the Church, and many people lump the ministry of a psalmist and that of a worship leader together. However, it's not true that they are the same. A psalmist and a worship leader have two different functions and require different giftings. Just because someone is a great worship leader doesn't mean that person is a psalmist—or vice versa.

A worship leader is a musician who leads others in worshiping God—but a psalmist is a minister who sings sermons and preaches songs! Each time the psalmist ministers, or even picks up a musical instrument, the anointing of God comes on him to preach, which is not what happens with a worship leader.

How else is a psalmist different? First, a psalmist's words flow directly out of his spirit by the power of the Holy Spirit. When people come to a service and are hungry for God, the Spirit of God draws things out of the psalmist according to what those people need. God knows who needs what, and He is the Master Planner of meeting needs.

Because of these different needs, Holy Spirit may use the psalmist to teach on many different subjects in one service. It may seem topically as though the psalmist is jumping all over the place, yet this approach allows God to minister to everyone. A teacher, on the other hand, typically explains the Word of God systematically, line upon line and precept upon precept. He builds a foundation layer by layer.

God placed the fivefold offices in the Church for varied purposes, as we see in 1 Corinthians 12:1–3. In speaking of spiritual gifts, the Bible tells us there are "diversities of gifts" (v. 4 KJV), "differences of administrations" (v. 5 KJV), and "diversities of operations" (v. 6 KJV), but they all originate with God. The teacher is one of the fivefold gifts, whereas the ministry of the psalmist and the worship leader fall under the ministry of helps (v. 28).

Because there is an element of prophecy to what he does, a psalmist must spend considerable time separated from others, in that secret place with God, praying, listening, and worshiping (1 Cor. 14:14). The truths revealed during these times with God are what the psalmist releases by the Holy Spirit when he ministers.

I have found this to be true in my own life. When I pick up my guitar, or begin singing, or even quoting a Scripture-based song, the Holy Spirit stirs up truth from my spirit, it crosses through my brain, and I minister God-realities relevant to those present. That's because I'm a psalmist.

God told me I was a psalmist when I was forty-two years old. He told me that He had anointed me, but that until then, I had buried my talents in the earth (through soulish music).

When He told me this, I asked him, "God, would You take the Word and show me what You are doing in me? Please show me."

He said, “Go read the Psalms. Just as David was a prophet and a psalmist in the youth of his ministry, so are you.”

Then the Holy Spirit explained to me, “If you are going to have My life run off you, son, you must live a life separate from the world, as well as guard who you allow to be your friend. Do not let everyone be a friend to you. Protect your calling, as I am going to put you in other offices.” And that is exactly what He’s done.

Another important truth about psalmists is that they are not all musically inclined. But those who are put what they are hearing from God to music. This is basically what the psalmist David did in the Old Testament, as did other psalmists mentioned throughout the poetic books of the Old Testament.

In general, a psalmist:

- hears the voice of the Holy Spirit in his spirit.
- yields to the Holy Spirit.
- hears fresh revelation from God as he ministers.
- flows in a prophetic anointing, fulfilling the office of the prophet.

Many people—and even many preachers—do not recognize the psalmist’s ministry. However, 1 Chronicles

25:1 says the psalmist David appointed singers and praisers unto the Lord, and that these men had certain anointings and giftings to "prophesy with harps, with psalteries, and with cymbals" (KJV). The ministry of a psalmist is still the same today!

A dear friend of mine and a psalmist, David Ingles, gives a great example of a psalmist in one of his songs entitled "You Are Free":[3]

As I look at you, the love of God within me
Rises from my spirit to my voice.
His holy love is flowing to you through me
While I pronounce the words of God's own choice.
It's compassion I obtained from Jesus
The Holy Spirit's demonstrating way:
The power of God to birth, to heal, deliver
Is declared a fact of faith today.

When traveling throughout the United States, I functioned as a psalmist, which gives place to the prophetic anointing. And while ministering, I operated in the gifts of the Spirit associated with the prophetic office: the word of wisdom, the word of knowledge, and the discerning of spirits (1 Cor. 12:8, 10).

Now, just because I prophesied, it does not mean that I (or any other psalmist) am a prophet. It only means the anointing of the Holy Spirit was upon me to prophesy.

The General Gift of Psalming

Although a psalmist is someone called to public ministry, the gift of psalming is for every believer:

> ***Speaking to yourselves in psalms and hymns and spiritual songs, singing and making melody in your heart to the Lord.***
>
> —Ephesians 5:19 KJV

> ***Let the word of Christ dwell in you richly in all wisdom; teaching and admonishing one another in psalms and hymns and spiritual songs, sing with grace in your hearts to the Lord.***
>
> —Colossians 3:16 KJV

In these two passages from the writings of the apostle Paul, we see the Spirit of God admonishing all believers to "psalm" (as an action) in our devotional lives *and* in corporate settings. This begins when someone is tender to the Spirit, and they hear a phrase or a few words. If they step into that anointing and yield to the Spirit, they will bring forth the psalm they hear. This may occur at home after a season of prayer or a devotional time or in a public setting. By psalming, a believer edifies and exhorts whoever is listening. If he is alone, a believer builds himself up.

A good comparison of the operation of psalming is what happens when a believer hears a thought or a few words from the indwelling Spirit, and then, by faith, he speaks them out in prophecy or while preaching. A person who psalms unto the Lord has heard God speak to him on the inside—in his spirit. The Spirit of the Lord echoes a word unto him because "for as many as are led by the Spirit of God, they are the sons of God" (Rom. 8:14 KJV).

The Psalmist's Ministry Requires Yielding to the Spirit

We are all called to yield to God and follow Holy Spirit's leading. However, if a person has the anointing of a psalmist, and is equipped with this gift, it means they have learned to yield to the Spirit of God with a greater anointing and with regularity.

For believers to become more yielded, I encourage them to get up every morning and say, "Good morning, Holy Ghost! You are welcome in this place! Do Your work in me!" I speak those words every morning, and so have other great men and women of God. Smith Wigglesworth started every single morning by praying and dancing in the

Holy Ghost for fifteen minutes. That is how he kept himself conscious and yielded to the Greater One who lived in him.

We learn to yield to Holy Ghost in our day-to-day experiences by being God-inside conscious and walking with Him. Starting out with Him in the morning goes a long way toward making that happen. If we want to be more yielded, we need to allow our spirits to dominate instead of our flesh. In other words, rolling out of bed instead of rolling over to sleep fifteen more minutes will take us to another level in life!

Chapter Three

The True Worshipers

God is a Spirit: and they that worship him must worship him in spirit and in truth.

—John 4:24

What is spiritual worship? How do we worship in spirit and in truth? I hope to answer these questions in this chapter. The apostle John shares that it became a concern of Jesus that the new breed of people who would follow Him were to worship in spirit and in truth. Much of our worship in the twenty-first century majors on soulish worship instead of spiritual worship.

In John 4, Jesus explained true worship. Jesus had left Judea and was on His way to Galilee. The route He had chosen took Him through Samaria, and in so doing, He sat down to rest at Jacob's well, which was in Samaria. There came a woman of Samaria, and Jesus began to speak with her. After a short conversation with Jesus, this Samaritan woman began asking Him about the best place of worship. She was a Samaritan, and He was a Jew. The Jews and Samaritans were at odds with each other, and they had each long since designated different locations to be *the* correct place of worship.

> *There cometh a woman of Samaria to draw water: Jesus saith unto her, Give me to drink. (For his disciples were gone away unto the city to buy meat.) Then saith the woman of Samaria unto him, How is it that thou, being a Jew, askest drink of me, which am a woman of Samaria? for the Jews have no dealings with the Samaritans. Jesus answered and said unto her, if thou knewest the gift of God, and who it is that saith to thee, Give me to drink; thou wouldest have asked of him, and he would have given thee living water. The woman saith unto him, Sir, thou hast nothing to draw with, and the well is deep: from whence then hast thou that living water? Art thou greater than our father Jacob, which gave us the well, and drank thereof himself, and*

his children, and his cattle? Jesus answered and said unto her, Whosoever drinketh of this water shall thirst again: But whosoever drinketh of the water that I shall give him shall never thirst; but the water that I shall give him shall be in him a well of water springing up into everlasting life. Jesus saith unto her, Go, call thy husband, and come hither. The woman answered and said, I have no husband. Jesus said unto her, Thou hast well said, I have no husband: For thou hast had five husbands; and he whom thou now hast is not thy husband: in that saidst thou truly. The woman saith unto him, Sir, I perceive that thou art a prophet. Our fathers worshipped in this mountain; and ye say, that in Jerusalem is the place where men ought to worship. Jesus saith unto her, Woman, believe me, the hour cometh, when ye shall neither in this mountain, nor yet at Jerusalem, worship the Father. Ye worship ye know not what: we know what we worship: for salvation is of the Jews. But the hour cometh, and now is, when the true worshippers shall worship the Father in spirit and in truth: for the Father seeketh such to worship him. God is a Spirit: and they that worship him must worship him in spirit and in truth. The woman saith unto him, I know that Messias cometh, which is called Christ: when he is come, he will tell us all things. Jesus saith unto her, I that speak unto thee am he.

—John 4:7–26

In John 4:23–24, Jesus gave her a revelation of things to come. He said, "But the hour cometh, and now is, when the true worshippers shall worship the Father in spirit and in truth: for the Father seeketh such to worship him. God is a Spirit: and they that worship him must worship him in spirit and in truth" (KJV).

This word Jesus brought to this Samaritan woman was foretelling the manner of worship for the Church of Jesus Christ. At that time, no one had been born again, since Jesus had not gone to the cross yet. Once a person experiences the new birth and becomes alive unto God, they can worship God *in the Spirit*. Even today, two thousand years after Jesus paid for our redemption, many people confuse the spirit and the soul. This is mostly due to incorrect teaching of the Word of God. However, the Bible is clear that man is a threefold being. Man is a spirit; he possesses a soul; and he is housed in a body. In 1 Thessalonians 5:23, we see the threefold man clearly revealed: "And the very God of peace sanctify you wholly; and I pray God your whole spirit and soul and body be preserved blameless unto the coming of our Lord Jesus Christ" (KJV). Hebrews 4:12 further clarifies, "For the word of God is quick, and powerful, and sharper than any twoedged sword, piercing even to the dividing asunder of soul and spirit, and of the joints and marrow, and is a discerner of the thoughts and intents of the heart" (KJV). God is a Spirit, and for the Father to receive our worship, it must be given in the Spirit.

God created man as a spirit, made in His image and likeness. Just as He is a Spirit, we, too, are spirits. Both soulish worship and physical worship were acceptable in the Old Testament because the people were not born again at that time. They did not have the life and nature of God within them. Hebrews 8:6 tells us that in the New Covenant Jesus instituted, "He is the mediator of a better covenant, which was established upon better promises" (KJV). So, our worship in the New Covenant is "better" and at a higher spiritual level. Jesus reinstates our position with God, so we can fellowship with the Father like Adam did before he sinned in the Garden of Eden—Spirit to spirit.

Learning what our worship songs mean and what they are saying empowers us to worship God at a higher spiritual level and in greater purity and truth. For worship to be its purest and highest, we must know (exactly and precisely) what the words of a song means. This is crucial to our worship! So, examine your songs to determine if they fulfill the truth of God's Word.

For an example, let's look at the song "Garment of Praise." In Isaiah 61:1–3, the prophet Isaiah was prophesying to the forthcoming Church that Jesus was bringing a new and living way. Zion is a type of the Church. Joy is to replace mourning and sorrow. God authorized and directed Isaiah to proclaim liberty to the Jews in Babylon. This passage carried a double meaning, also referencing Jesus and His future Church. Jesus repeated these words in the Jewish synagogue in Nazareth, applying these words to Himself and to the upcoming Church. Verse 1 of the song "Garment of Praise" declares:[4]

All you that mourn in Zion
I have authority
To appoint unto you in Zion
Oil of joy that will set you free.

You see, God does not want believers mourning. For our mourning and sorrow, according to Isaiah 61:3, He appointed the oil of joy. Oil represents the Holy Spirit. Holy Spirit will give you joy in place of mourning. God gives to us the garment of praise for the spirit of heaviness, as the lyrics of this song tell us. This simply means it is a choice or a decision to praise God. Choosing to praise God is an act of our will. Most of the time, praise is not automatic. In 1 Corinthians 14:15, the Bible tells the believer to pray with the spirit and with the understanding. Since praise is the highest kind of prayer, we could say that we praise with the spirit and with the understanding.

In John 4:24, Jesus told the Samaritan woman at the well that the Lord is looking for those who worship in spirit and in truth. He told her that the Samaritans did not know who they worshiped. He then said that those who worship the Father *must* worship in spirit and in truth. *Must* is a strong word of obligation, requirement, or duty. If you and I are going to worship the Father, we *must* worship Him in spirit and in truth for it to qualify as worship to God.

It is not just enough to have words of truth paired with worldly music. Does the music sound like the world? We need the right spirit in our music, coupled with the truth of the Word of God, specifically the Pauline epistles, with which to worship the Father. We learn from John 17:17 that God's Word is truth. So, we should be declaring the Word of God in our worship unto Him.

When I traveled throughout the United States, I crisscrossed America many times singing the Word of God and seeing miracles. If you want to see miracles, signs, and wonders, you must sing out of the spirit, not out of the soul (your mind, will, and emotions). Most music, including congregational worship today, ministers out of the soul to the people. Soulish worship focuses on man—how people feel and how they express their emotions. On the other hand, spiritual worship in a church service should be ministry to God, and it should be done in the spirit. Much of our music today ministers to people, *not* to God.

Someone recently asked a Pentecostal old-timer, "What are we missing in this twenty-first-century move of God?" He replied, "The Church spends little to no time in its worship services singing in other tongues." We recall that the gift of tongues is the doorway to all the gifts of the Spirit. Thus, our purpose should focus on bringing about the edification by God of His people, the Church. By majoring on spiritual development, the overflow of God affects and refreshes the mind and body as well as the spirit.

Chapter Four

Understanding the Flow of the Holy Spirit

If we live in the Spirit, let us also walk in the Spirit.

—GALATIANS 5:25 KJV

SPIRITUAL THINGS ARE MUCH LIKE NATURAL THINGS. THERE is a training or learning curve. As pastors, teachers, and worship leaders, it is vital to know when the Spirit of God is speaking prophetically through an individual in the Church. Without leaders who understand the move of God, services will get out of hand, confusion will set in, and people's lives can be damaged. Knowing how to direct a service by understanding what is happening in the Spirit is paramount to keeping spiritual order in a service.

In 1 Corinthians 14, Paul tells us not to allow a message to be spoken forth in tongues without an interpreter. Confusion and chaos happen in a service where there is utterance without direction and spiritual leadership. Paul addresses disorder in the Corinthian church due to this very issue. In fact, much of the book of Corinthians addresses this. Clarity, understanding, true leadership, and spiritual discernment are necessary to keep order in the service and for the gift of tongues to reach its purpose, which is to edify, encourage, and strengthen the body. The goal and purpose of the vocal gifts in a service is the edifying of the Church (1 Cor. 14:26).

Many people who are untaught in spiritual things (or soulishly ruled) speak from their souls instead of their spirits. Quite frequently, immature believers—especially those who are young in the things of the Spirit—start out giving a prophecy in the soul, and then transition to the Spirit in bringing forth the message of God.

The Spirit of God is a perfect gentleman, and He works with us. His role is always to put Jesus and His followers over. We learn in the book of John that Jesus referred to the Holy Ghost as the Comforter; the Greek word He used is *paraclete* (14:16). Essentially Holy Spirit is called alongside of us to help us. He allows us to operate in the soul, knowing that even as born-again believers, we are still housed in flesh.

Many times an individual starts out prophesying from their soul, and then Holy Spirit directs them into the message He desires to bring. In 1 Corinthians 14:10, the Bible says there are many kinds of voices—none without significance. Each soul has a voice, as does each spirit.

Because we are humans with a mind, a will, and emotions, we may start a prophecy in the flesh and out of our soul before we get to the path God wants us to take. So often we start in the flesh, but Holy Spirit gently leads us into the Spirit, thus accomplishing His purpose and His intent. We thank God for the grace of God!

Understanding what is happening in each phase of a worship service and ministry to God is required in order to flow with Holy Spirit. Here is a graphic to help understand and simplify the spiritual order of worship. A picture is worth a thousand words.

1. When the Holy Spirit uses a pastor or teacher to preach to and teach a congregation of people, this teaching ministry comes from God, descending to

the earth to the people as marked by the downward arrow ↓.

2. When the congregation worships God, singing psalms, hymns, and spiritual songs as it is described in Ephesians 5:19, then the ministry is moving from earth to heaven. It is flowing from the people and ascending back up to God. This is reflected in the upward arrow ↑.
3. God wants to minister to His people, transitioning the ministry from heaven back down to earth ↓. This occurs through a ministry gift, or a believer operating in the gifts of the Spirit, such as prophecy or the gift of tongues and the gift of interpretation.

HEAVEN TO EARTH—EARTH TO HEAVEN—HEAVEN TO EARTH

Holy Ghost is the Conductor of worship. He operates through human leaders. The more accurately the ministry team flows with Holy Spirit, the more profoundly God will move in our services and in our lives. Joy should permeate every service. If we sing the Word of God to the Lord, it builds up and edifies our spirit, and joy manifests!

When I was traveling and ministering in the office of prophet/psalmist, all the profit of the traveling ministry went for missions. Although I never talked about missions, the Holy Spirit flowed money through my hands. Jesus is the only One who changes us. As a psalmist, I preached Jesus, and what was the result? People experienced the joy of the Lord. They would get drunk in the Holy Ghost singing this new-creation music. It is powerful and anointed! It is the Word of God put to musical score. And it produces signs and wonders.

How do you know when a prophecy is from God? If the prophetic utterance lines up with the teaching that occurred during the service, there is a harmonious flow and continuity in the Spirit. If the minister taught on faith, the prophecy should reinforce the message of faith. For example, if the teaching in the service was on prayer, the exhortation and encouragement from the Spirit of God will be regarding prayer and communion with God. Holy Spirit hooks up with you. He brings continuity to the service.

After singing the Word of God and ministering to the Lord in psalms, hymns, and spiritual songs, the congregation should wait quietly in God's presence for a few minutes and allow God to speak edification, exhortation, and comfort through the vocal gifts of the Spirit.

Timing is key in a move of the Spirit. A prophecy that is out of order loses its impact. An ill-timed or ill-placed prophecy is out of order simply because it should have occurred elsewhere in the service. It does not mean the prophecy is not from God. It simply needed to be given at a different time in the service in order to reap the greatest benefit. I will elaborate more on the moving of the Spirit in later chapters.

Chapter Five

New Creation Music and Its Importance

Therefore if any man be in Christ, he is a new creature: old things are passed away; behold all things are become new.

—2 CORINTHIANS 5:17 KJV

MANY OF THE OLD HYMNS, AND MUCH OF THE CHURCH music today, is based more in emotion than it is based in Scripture. These songs talk about how great life becomes once we get to heaven, but here on earth there's only sickness and suffering. And then there are the songs about mom and her prayers that can even make us cry.

However, songs that are unscriptural or based solely on emotion do not glorify God. They talk about who we were before we met the Anointed One, Christ Jesus, and that doesn't create faith. It brings unbelief. That unbelief then robs believers of their faith instead of strengthening them. If there is no faith in their hearts when they have a crisis, they will not have anything in their spirits to move a mountain (of trouble), and God will not be glorified.

According to 2 Corinthians 5:17, if you are in Christ, you are a new creation, and old things—the old man and nature—have passed away. In Colossians 1:13, the apostle Paul tells us that we have been "delivered...from the power of darkness, and translated into the kingdom of his dear Son" (KJV). At the new birth, the nature of God replaces our old satanic nature. Jesus told us in John 10:10 that in giving us a new nature, He came to give us life and life more abundantly. We can search the Scriptures, specifically those in the letters to the Church, to learn who we have become as new creations in Christ. The life that Christ bought for us is a life of victory and winning on earth *now* through the substitutionary work of Jesus Christ on the cross.

All throughout the New Testament, we learn that each believer has a life that Christ bought for us through His substitutionary work on the cross! Wouldn't that be better to sing about?

You Are the Total of Your Talking Yesterday

In Philemon 1:6, the apostle Paul exhorts us, "That the communication of thy faith may become effectual by the acknowledging of every good thing which is in you in Christ Jesus" (KJV). The proclamation or admonition from Scripture throughout the Word is to continually acknowledge who we are in Christ Jesus. This involves not just making a good confession occasionally by acknowledging a scripture. No, this is to be our manner of life. There must be a continuous pattern of speaking, reading, singing, and talking about who we are in Christ if we are to have the power of God in our daily life as well as in moments of crisis (Josh. 1:8).

The Bible says in Proverbs 18:21, "Death and life are in the power of the tongue: and they that love it shall eat the fruit thereof" (KJV). People build their lives by the words they speak every day. You are the total of your talking yesterday.

Perhaps problems assail you, and you then voice these issues to others. However, if you sit down and analyze what came out of your mouth yesterday, you may very well see how today you were snared and taken captive by the words of your mouth that you spoke the day before (Prov. 6:2). In short, you will see the reason for your problems today by examining the words you spoke in the past. The only way you are going to make your tomorrow better is to change your conversation and change your words today.

Do you realize that you are a spirit; you have a soul; and you live in a body? Remember, your spirit does not sleep. If you wake up in the morning and there's a scriptural song running around in you all day, it's because your spirit rehearsed that song during the night. It crept over into your mind upon waking, but it really came out of your spirit. Faith comes out of your spirit because that is where faith works. Faith is a spiritual force, and it resides in your spirit. God's Word coming out of your spirit positions you for His blessings.

The Power of Faith-Filled Words

In my first pastorate at Living Water Teaching, new creation songs—faith-filled songs from Scripture or the Spirit—formed much of our music. Just as the Jews in the Old Testament rehearsed who God was and what He had done for them, we followed the same pattern in our church by singing about what Jesus accomplished at Calvary for us. Here is an example of a faith-building song entitled "Our King of Kings":[5]

Verse 1:

When life tries to crowd you with doubting

And reason is doubt in disguise

You hold the key to the kingdom

Sing out, and faith will arise.

Chorus:

Kings and priests, He made us to be

We have what we say

We get what we see

Faith is the victory, and love is the key

Jesus is Lord and our King of kings.

Verse 2:

We wrestle not against flesh and blood

But principalities and powers up high

But the greater One is within me

And He's living big in me now.

Do you see the power in these words, taken directly from the Word of God? If I broke down this song by displaying the various referenced scriptures, you would see that we are simply singing the Word of God. Singing the Word changes the outcome of your life!

One man who attended Living Water Teaching once fell off a ladder and seriously hurt his arm. Later, he shared something profound with me. He said that because we sang new creation songs in church, when he fell and was lying there on the ground, the words of our songs came to him. He said, "The overcoming, Word-filled music kept rising in my spirit. It just kept rising and rising."

When he fell, he did not say, "Woe is me! I will never work again!" Instead, while he was riding to the hospital in the ambulance, he started singing these words: "In Him I live and move and have my being; I'm a new creature in Christ, and with joy I sing. His life, His love, His nature, and His ability are mine as I reign in life in Him!"

The doctors told him he would only gain a small percentage of the use of his arm back. Within a few days, though, he had regained the complete use of his hand and elbow. In two weeks, the doctors took off the cast, and he was fine.

This man got his spiritual bucket bumped, but because he had been filling his spirit and mind with God's Word, what he was full of splashed out. He was the total of what he had been saying (and singing). In this case, it was faith that he put in, and faith came out when he needed it the most.

If you sing, read, and quote the Word of God, it keeps you tuned to the Spirit. The Word of God goes into your eye gate, comes out of your mouth, and back into your ear gate. When it does, it drops into your spirit from your mouth. When it comes out of your spirit, it then becomes your *rhema*, bubbling up into life and blessing (Deut. 30:19). It will move the mountain, and it will dry up the roots of the fig tree—just like Jesus said.

Renewing Your Mind Through Songs

Singing words of faith and victory to yourself over and over builds an aura of confidence. The Bible says, "This is the victory that overcometh the world, even our faith" (1 John 5:4 KJV). When you build up confidence with Scriptures like that, you'll find yourself singing songs like "Satan Has Been Paralyzed":[6]

The devil is a blabbermouth
Distorting every fact
But the truth is, he's a loser
Since Jesus broke his back.

Most people learn just enough about faith to get into trouble. They go around *hearing* about faith, but they never walk in faith because they never feed on the Word regularly. Without systematically feeding on the Word, they do not get enough heart-faith to walk victoriously. Then, when a crisis comes, these same believers need someone else to do their praying and believing for them. There is no overcoming victory there.

When some people get saved, they say unscriptural things like, "I am a dirty, old worm and a sinner saved by grace." What is wrong with believers saying they are sinners? It is double-minded. They are basing their salvation on how they feel or on man's tradition, not God's Word!

I am not a sinner saved by grace. I used to be a sinner, but now I am a new creation! I used to be a dirty, old worm, but now I am El Shaddai Jr.! Why would I go around saying, "I'm only a sinner saved by grace"? *No!* I am *not* a sinner. I am a new creation in Christ Jesus! I no longer identify with Satan and sin; I now identify with Christ and all the provisions and benefits that come with being in that position! Why? Because that's what the Word of God says about me.

Sticking to the Word of God

Over the years, many people have said that I am too narrow-minded. If they think I am narrow-minded, just wait until they stand before Jesus! Jesus said, "I am the way, the truth, and the life: no man cometh unto the Father, but by me" (John 14:6 KJV). You cannot get any more narrow-minded than that!

So, why would you not stick to the Word of God? As a minister of the Gospel, why would you preach the Word and then sing unbelief or only your feelings or emotions? Why would you get in those old, moldy hymnbooks and in every third verse sing the traditions of men? Your mama might have taught you that song, but so what? I love my mama, too. She prayed me into the ministry. But that doesn't mean I'd sing a song about unbelief just because she taught it to me!

The Wilderness without the Word

God has set every believer on a course that goes from the new birth to the promised land. But there is always a wilderness experience in between the two. When you got up the next morning after you were born again, the devil might have told you your salvation was not real. That is what happened to me. The next morning after my new birth, I still wanted a cigarette and girls still did not get ugly. You might have had the same kind of wilderness experience when you got up the next morning after your own salvation experience. Why did that happen? Our bodies (our flesh) was not born again; only our spirit man was born again.

That night my spirit was born again. I became a new creation, but I still had to get my salvation worked out until my flesh lined up with God's Word. Furthermore, my thoughts, my mind, and my tongue had to line up with what happened that night, and that took renewing my mind with the Word of God.

I really wanted to go to heaven the morning after I got born again. I did not think I could live out the Christian life. I had no faith for living out a victorious Christian life. I thought, *God, this would be a good time to go to heaven. I won't have to sin anymore.* I did not know anything about a victorious life—did you?

For the first twenty years of my life, all I preached was sin. Do you know what is sad? Some ministers are still preaching sin. If you preach sin, it will make you and all your congregation sin-conscious. Satan wants to keep people aware of their flesh and past sins, so they will question if they are even saved.

We know that salvation is the work of God, not man. We had nothing to do with it except saying yes to Jesus. Besides, our sin is eliminated from the mind of God, so it should be eliminated from ours, too. In Hebrew 10:17, God says, "And their sins and iniquities will I remember no more" (KJV).

We see God's provision for the Israelites in Psalm 105:37–43 while they traveled through the desert on their way to the promised land. He always provides, even in the wilderness of life. This is a song we sing in my church based on those Scriptures:

Chorus:

He brought forth His people with joy.

He brought forth His people with joy.

His chosen with gladness

He brought forth His people with joy.

Verse:

He brought them forth with silver and with gold.

And there was not one feeble among their tribe.

He spread a cloud for a covering and a fire to give light in the night.

He opened up the rock, and the waters gushed out like a river in dry places.

This psalm is also a picture of the Church of Jesus Christ. So, if this is true, why are we ever "in the wilderness"? Because every time we miss God with our mouths, we take another lap around the mountain.

Some believers have been in the wilderness for forty years, just like the Israelites. Most of the Israelites never entered the promised land. Believers can get delivered from their sins and be born again and still miss all the goodness and provision Jesus bought for them at Calvary! They will miss it if they do not renew their minds to what belongs to them in Christ.

So, how do you stop taking laps around the mountain? By changing the songs you currently sing to one like this, entitled "The Song of the Lord":[7]

I will sing unto the Lord forever
For He hath overcome gloriously
The horse and the rider hath He cast into the sea
The Lord is my strength and song.

Chorus:

The song of the Lord is on His people
The battle cry, the war dance of victory
Sing, O Zion, sing, tho' in a strange land
The song of the Lord, redeemed.

What determines the length of your stay in the wilderness is what comes out of your mouth. When you sing songs like the one above, you can move through the wilderness and into the promised land more quickly. What you speak forth from your mouth determines how long you will stay in the wilderness. You are the total of your talking yesterday.

I had to quit singing many songs because there was no faith coming out of my mouth. Faith must be released in both our words and singing, since this is what brings the Word to pass in our lives.

Pastors and teachers, the songs noted in this book can be great teaching tools. They are jam-packed with New Testament truths that believers everywhere must learn. Congregational songs should give people a glimpse of your doctrine, bringing continuity between the worship and the teaching in each service. Here's another new creation song that talks about singing the right things, entitled "I Don't Sing Those Songs Anymore":[8]

"Folsom Prison Blues" and "Mack the Knife"
Invite the chains of bondage and of strife.
Don't think it's not important what you say, 'cause today
You're the total of your talking yesterday.
Now I sing, "The Seed of Abraham"
The righteousness of God, that's who I am.
Things in life just started working out
When I stopped singing songs that peddle death and doubt.

Chorus:

I don't sing those songs anymore
Like "born to lose," and of the life before
What we say is what we get for sure
I don't sing those songs anymore.

The third verse in this song talks about how we are the seed of Abraham (Gal. 3:29) and the righteousness of God in Christ through the new birth of the spirit. These are two important biblical truths to sing.

> *But what saith it? The word is nigh thee, even in thy mouth, and in thy heart: that is, the word of faith, which we preach; that if thou shalt confess with thy mouth the Lord Jesus, and shalt believe in thine heart that God hath raised him from the dead, thou shalt be saved.*
>
> —ROMANS 10:8–9 KJV

The word "saved" here comes from a Greek word, *sozo*, which implies the new birth of the human spirit, the blessing of physical healing, and the deliverance from worry, mental heaviness, and oppression. The definition also includes soundness, safety, preservation, health, welfare, and prosperity.

We who are saved are new creations in Christ. We are re-created ones, made in the image of God, and we spiritually look like our Master. We have become "partakers of God's divine nature" (2 Pet. 1:4 KJV). We are the Church of the Lord Jesus Christ. He is the Head, and the Church is His body.

By singing new creation music to the Lord in your prayer closet or in a corporate setting, you are depositing faith into your spirit. The Bible says in Romans 10:17, "Faith cometh by hearing, and hearing by the word of God" (KJV).

If you want to move mountains in your life by flowing with God, it requires faith. Hebrews 11:1 tells us, "Faith is the substance of things hoped for, the evidence of things not seen" (KJV). In Hebrews 11:6, we read, "Without faith it is impossible to please [God]" (KJV). This means that singing songs without faith does not please God, either. I want my words, my thoughts, and my entire life to please God, don't you?

By singing songs of faith and new creation truths, it stirs up the Holy Spirit because He is the distributor of signs and wonders Himself. In the gospels, Jesus told His disciples that upon His departure from earth to heaven, where He would perform His high priestly ministry, as they preached the Gospel of the Kingdom—new creation realities—signs and wonders would accompany them (Mark 16:15–20). Also, in Hebrews 2:4, this same message is clear: "God also bearing them witness, both with signs and wonders, and with divers miracles, and gifts of the Holy Ghost, according to his own will" (KJV).

Arlene Reitz, a missionary from Guatemala with Living Water Teaching, once gave this prophecy during a teaching and demonstration of the power of singing new creation realities:

> *I say unto you, my sons and my daughters, you are the seed of Abraham. You are being planted even now in*

good ground. You will see much fruit manifested from this time you have been called here together. This time is truly ordained of Me. As you have listened with your inner ears and have sung these songs with learned tongues, they have been written on your heart, and you will never be the same. You will remember these words, for I will call them to your remembrance by My Holy Spirit.

As you take these words and sing them in your homes, they will be filled with My presence. Healing will be manifested in your bodies, and your marriages will be healed. Bondages will be broken, and relationships will be restored by the anointing of these words. And as you sing them in your churches, you will see many come to Jesus. And by His power and His presence, you will see signs and wonders as you confess and sing My Word. For these are My Words! You are appointed by Me to sing them. Be obedient and yield to My Holy Spirit and His direction, and I will open the doors to hearts of many. Many will come and be set free and brought from the kingdom of darkness into the Kingdom of light through My dear Son.

New Testament prophecy confirms what God is saying through the ministry gifts. This prophetic message certainly exhorted and encouraged the people and confirmed the Word being taught during the Psalminar, and it is a prophetic word to the Church today.

Another truth to sing about is how the Word works when it is applied to a situation. Here is a song based on a testimony of someone being raised from the dead, entitled "(Go Back), She's Using That Name":[9]

There's a story that's been told us

How a man left this life

Two precious children, one loving wife

Angels carried him over the tide

He wanted to stay there, but an angel replied.

Chorus:

"You'll have to go back,

She's using that name,

Although you'd love to stay

You'll just have to wait.

All things are possible

And prayer's made a change,

You'll have to go back,

She's using that name."

Verse 2:

Looking down from heaven there in the hall,

His love was praying,

That name she called,

An angel turned to him

And this he explained:
"You're welcome to be here,
But she's using that name."

Verse 3:

That name has power
And death knows it well.
Jesus is Lord of lords
Over death, grave, and hell.
Believers have authority
The Word makes it plain
To speak life to the lifeless in Jesus' name.

Before I even learned this song, I had seen God raise my older brother, Don, from the dead! It was many years ago, and my younger brother, Jim, and I were the only ones in our family who were filled with the Holy Spirit. My family had left strict orders at the hospital not to let Jim and me in because they thought we would pray for Don's healing. (They did not want us disturbing things.) However, we snuck in the back door of the hospital and went up the back stairway. We did not know it then, but Don was already dead.

When we asked the hospital staff where he was, they directed us to his room. Jim and I found where his body lay with a sheet over him. They were about to transfer him to an area to prepare him for burial.

Back then, I only had an inkling of faith, but when Jim and I found him, we began speaking faith over him. We walked around the room praying in other tongues even though we were young in the baptism of the Holy Ghost. I remembered the words of Jesus in John 11:25 and quoted those over his body: "Though [a man] were dead, yet shall he live" (KJV). As we prayed in tongues again, suddenly Don sat up and looked at us!

Don sat there and told Jim and me that he had left his body and had watched us running across the hospital parking lot. He could see through all the floors of the hospital, and he could see all our family members crying.

Similarly, Brother Kenneth Hagin has shared his testimony of how, during a near-death experience, he could see his family members still on earth. Much scientific evidence describes similar occurrences when people return to their bodies after officially dying. In fact, medical training facilities have recognized the spiritual happenings in these instances and have begun to train doctors on how to call people back into their bodies during these near-death experiences.

Don told us that he went to heaven quickly. He described to us his walking across this beautiful green place in heaven. He said, "All of a sudden, I realized that there was this great, huge man right beside me, not saying a word but just walking everywhere I walked. And I realized I did not have to say anything to him. I just knew that if I wanted to turn here, he knew it, and if he wanted to turn somewhere, I knew it without saying a word. And then I realized he was my angel. I had known him all my life."

While Don was in heaven, he saw our earthly father and spoke with him. Did you know that when you go to heaven, some of your family members will meet you there? Heaven will not be a shock to you. Jesus said in Matthew 24:35, "Heaven and earth shall pass away, but my words shall not pass away" (KJV).

Are you prepared to rule and reign with Jesus in heaven? Did you know that God tells us study and learning are necessary, both in heaven and earth? God told Joshua if he wanted to become prosperous and successful, he must meditate in the Word, day and night. You will continue to grow and learn in heaven. You see, there are no shortcuts to this life in the Spirit. We come into this world naturally as newborn babies, and our lives are continually filled with growing and learning. Spiritually, this is even more true. The apostle Paul admonished us in 2 Timothy 2:15: "Study to shew thyself approved unto God . . . rightly dividing the word of truth" (KJV).

There is no exhausting God and His truth. Science instructs us that the universe is continually expanding every second. God is the Master Creator. We are bid by Him to learn more and more and to become like Him. Heaven is a real place with real people. Truth is living and vital, and throughout all eternity, we will be learning and discovering more and more about God, ourselves, the universe, and His plans for us. We are the apple of His eye.

This is the reason I share Don's story. He entered heaven, and he was standing, holding hands with our earthly father. Don said, "All around me I could hear the name of Jesus reverberating throughout heaven." My earthly father said to him, "Don, there is that name, you cannot stay."

So, because we were using that name of Jesus in our prayers down on earth, my brother came right back from heaven! He said his angel escorted him from heaven, and he went back into his body in the hospital room, reentering his body through his mouth. Don's glorious experience affected our whole family.

When we sing about these kinds of truths, we build up our faith, and anything becomes possible.

Sing Faith–Preach Faith!

Jesus Christ walked on the earth as the Son of Man. He did not operate as the Son of God until He was raised from the dead as "the first-begotten of the dead" (Rev. 1:5 KJV). Oh yes, remember, Jesus left all the wealth and splendor of heaven to come to earth. Jesus became poor to make us rich (2 Cor. 8:9). He was cast out from the presence of God to make us welcome there. He wore a crown of thorns so that we could wear a crown of life.

As believers, we are to preach that Jesus died on the cross for our sins. However, the bearing of our sins is only part of the miraculous picture of the work of Christ for man. We must preach Jesus' great exchange. He became what we were so we could be and have what He is and has. We are made alive, righteous, strong, healed, and rich on earth—all because of the work of Christ, that is, the substitutionary work of Christ on the cross. It is your job and my job—ministers and laymen alike—to sing and preach this Gospel of Christ to the world.

If you do not sing and talk faith, faith will not be alive in you. Your mountain will not move out of the way, as Jesus told His disciples in Mark 11:23–24. If faith is alive in you, you will sing words of faith. Your music is the overflow of what you hide in your heart.

Many believers have been taught that they are unworthy sinners. This erroneous teaching inhibits believers from grasping their rights and privileges in Christ. However, in Christ, we are new creations; we are no longer sinners. That is, we have ceased to pursue a lifestyle of sin. We are admonished by the words of Hebrews 4:16: "Let us therefore come boldly unto the throne of grace, that we may obtain mercy, and find grace to help in time of need" (KJV). Every believer should walk in confidence and authority as overcomers.

As a result of this unworthiness (sin-consciousness) teaching, there is a common thread, or excuse, for not being and doing all that Jesus expects and commands. Christians who see themselves as unworthy worms in the dust do not think they are worthy to sing and preach God's Word. Yet, this is the deceptive lie the devil has fed the Church.

God mandates His Church to rule and reign in the earth. So, yes, it is your responsibility, Church, to sing and preach faith. Without it, you and I cannot please God (Heb. 11:6). Remember: "God [in Christ] is made unto us wisdom, and righteousness, and sanctification, and redemption" (1 Cor. 1:30 KJV). Jesus made us all the righteousness of God in Christ at salvation. We should be the first in line to share Christ, to take authority over the works of darkness wherever we find it, and to build the Kingdom of God. We should be in a footrace to be first in line to preach Christ and serve God!

We should be on fire for God, blazing with excitement and ready to do whatever is required to make an impact for Christ in our world. Jesus made us the righteousness of God in Christ. People say, "I am not really worthy. After all, God would never ask me to do that." When you know who you are in Christ, you will run through the line and say, "Me next, God!" And you will stand there excited and ready to work for God.

In my early days of pastoring, I had a church full of on-fire, Bible school students. I was almost intimidated that I might lose my place. I had a church full of young men and women who could outthink me and out-preach me. And yet, they were following me like I was Moses singing this music. I challenged, inspired, and encouraged my church members to be fanatics for Christ. I define a "fanatic" as a person who loves Jesus more than I do. I would rather have wildfire than no fire at all. Let's get fired up for God and preach everywhere we go. Let's light a fire in this world that can't be put out.

We are living in the New Covenant with a new set of instructions from Jesus. I am not knocking anyone's music. I am just encouraging the Church to go a little deeper with our music, so that a greater flow of God's revelation and gifts will manifest in our services and supernaturally meet the needs of the people. Like in the book of Jeremiah, we must sing the Word and watch what the Holy Ghost does:

> *Therefore they shall come and sing in the height of Zion,*
> *And shall flow together to the goodness of the LORD,*
> *for wheat, and for wine, and for oil, and for the young*
> *of the flock and of the herd*
> *and their soul shall be as a watered garden;*
> *and they shall not sorrow any more at all.*
>
> —JEREMIAH 31:12 KJV

Having a watered soul (or a renewed mind), as the song says, is a key to the glory of God manifesting in our churches and in our lives. We know the soul is our understanding (our will, mind, and emotions). Our souls are not the real us. The personality of the spirit is the real us. So, let's be the instruments of God. Be instant in season and out of season by feeding your spirit on the Word of God in every manner possible, and new creation realities will flow from you.

Chapter Six

The Fivefold Offices and Supportive Ministries

> *Humble yourselves therefore under the mighty hand of God, that he may exalt you in due time.*
>
> –1 PETER 5:6 KJV

IN THE EARLY CHURCH, THERE WERE TWO MINISTRY distinctives: the fivefold ministries (elders) and the supportive ministries (the deacons). We see the fivefold ministry listed in Ephesians 4:11–13 (KJV):

And he gave some, apostles; and some, prophets; and some, evangelists; and some, pastors and teachers; for the perfecting of the saints, for the work of the ministry, for the edifying of the body of Christ: Till we all come in the unity of the faith, and of the knowledge of the Son of God, unto a perfect man, unto the measure of the stature of the fulness of Christ.

In understanding the supportive ministries' role in the Church, we must look briefly at the first deacons and their function, as designated by the early Church.

As the Holy Spirit anointed the apostles of the Lamb to preach and teach, a great multiplication of both Jews and Greeks occurred. This overnight increase and success immediately resulted in a problem in the Church. The Greeks complained of neglect and discrimination in the food distribution, and so they brought the situation to the apostles. We find this story in Acts:

Then the twelve called the multitude of the disciples unto them, and said, It is not reason that we should leave the word of God, and serve tables. Wherefore, brethren, look ye out among you seven men of honest report, full of the Holy Ghost and wisdom, whom we may appoint over this business. But we will give ourselves continually to prayer, and to the ministry of the word. And the saying pleased the whole multitude: and they chose Stephen, a man full of faith and of the

> *Holy Ghost, and Philip, and Prochorus, and Nicanor, and Timon, and Parmenas, and Nicolas a proselyte of Antioch: Whom they set before the apostles: and when they had prayed, they laid their hands on them.*
>
> —ACTS 6:2–6 KJV

The apostolic leadership resolved the problems of this first disgruntled group in the Church by anointing other people who could stand in the gap and meet the needs of the members. In verse 4, the apostles were then able to "give [themselves] continually to prayer, and to the ministry of the word" (KJV). These first deacons served and assisted the fivefold ministry gifts in the Church as an extension of their authority.

Why Have the Fivefold Ministry?

> *And he gave some, apostles; and some, prophets; and some, evangelists; and some, pastors and teachers; for the perfecting of the saints, for the work of the ministry, for the edifying of the body of Christ: Till we all come in the unity of the faith, and of the knowledge of the Son of God, unto a perfect man, unto the measure of the stature of the fulness of Christ.*
>
> —EPHESIANS 4:11–13 KJV

Every minute, someone is born again. There are brand-new spiritual babies born into the Kingdom of God every day. If there are spiritual babies on the earth, then there must be people to help bring them to maturity. The function of the apostles, prophets, evangelists, pastors, and teachers is to bring these believers into spiritual manhood and the full development that is found in Christ. The job of the fivefold ministries is to train and equip the saints of God to serve as workers in the Kingdom of God.

The apostle Peter wrote in his first epistle that the fivefold ministry is the mighty hand of God in the earth, and that believers are to submit themselves "under the mighty hand of God, that he may exalt you in due time" (5:6 KJV).

Where should we find this expression of the fivefold ministry? In the local church.

A simple way to express the fivefold ministry is using the example of the hand.

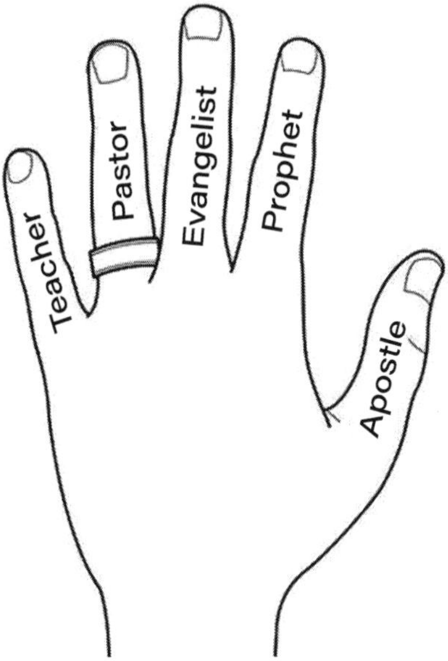

The index finger represents the prophet, who points his finger at everyone. The middle finger, the longest finger, depicts the function of the evangelist, who reaches the farthest to bring lost souls into the Kingdom. The little finger represents the teacher, because it can reach inside to tickle the ear and wipe out the sleepy bugs in the eyes. The ring finger illustrates the function of the pastor, because he loves, commits, and marries. He gives himself to the flock.

When you fold your fingers into your hand and wrap the thumb around them, the thumb depicts the apostle—the one who holds the church together. The apostle always sets things in order. He establishes the church, and he may temporarily pastor the church. The gift of the apostle houses each of the fivefold ministry operations, and he can function in each role as the need arises. None of the gifts, including the apostle, stand in the full measure of the Spirit, except Jesus, the Head of the Church.

Fivefold Ministry

As followers of Jesus, when we submit ourselves under the mighty hand of God—that is, under the fivefold ministry in the earth—God exalts us in due time. Many Bible school students set out to teach and minister the Word right out of Bible school; however, without having submitted to a fivefold ministry in a local church, they are still inexperienced in ministry.

Maturing in God involves more than learning the Word of God. In the book of Ephesians, Paul addresses marriage, admonishing husbands and wives to submit to each other, and in many other circumstances, the Bible instructs believers to lay down their wills to the will of another. Submission develops character. Biblical enlightenment alone cannot bring this to pass. It requires rubbing elbows with others in the Body of Christ, bowing your knee to a leader or fellow church member, keeping your mouth shut, and being willing to mold and change.

This sounds hard, but anyone in church or business knows this is mandatory in order for a person to develop and grow into a qualified, anointed leader. Without this molding and maturing process, impulsive and immature leaders will emerge, and ultimately hurt and crush the sheep for life. That is why Paul told Timothy not to put a novice in a position of leadership (1 Tim. 3:6). The edges of new leaders need to be worn off a bit, and they need to learn valuable lessons in dealing with people. These are essentials for those in a fivefold ministry position.

Fivefold Ministry versus Forefront Ministry: Is There a Difference?

Early in my ministry, God told me that the *forefront* ministry of helps is a supply line. The *fivefold* ministry is the frontline troops on the battle line. If an enemy wanted to win a battle, they would sever the opposing side's connection between the battle line and the supply line. Both are mandatory for winning battles. This is true both naturally and spiritually.

Before I attended Rhema Bible Training Center, the only ministry gifts mentioned in churches in which I attended or ministered were the pastor and the missionary. In fact, I had never even heard of the ministry of helps until I attended Rhema. The church world in which I was involved expected the pastor to do everything. Many times, this is why pastors quit the ministry and churches shut down—they are simply burned out.

As I attended Bible school, I learned from the Word of God about the fivefold offices of apostle, prophet, evangelist, pastor, and teacher. Earlier we learned how the Holy Ghost developed the role of deacons to support the fivefold ministry in the book of Acts. This way, the fivefold ministers could spend their time teaching and ministering to the people through the study of the Word of God and prayer.

Even as the early Church expanded and grew, men and women performed other supporting duties, such as outreach ministry to the widows and to the poor. We see by this it was Holy Ghost who introduced the ministry of helps in the early Church as a guide for us to follow.

So, who fulfills the *forefront* ministry? A deacon serving in a forefront position serves the pastor just like any other person serving in the ministry of helps. However, a forefront role means this person is very visible to others. They could be the worship leader, singers, musicians, prayer leaders, ushers, or greeters, to name a few.

Individuals who are extremely visible in the ministry of helps to the congregation are referred to as "forefront" ministers. This can make it easy for them to feel a sense of entitlement and think they are more important than others. But this mindset is a clear indication they are still a novice.

The world system is all about self-promotion and self-exaltation; however, true believers find their security and confidence in knowing they are the righteousness of God. They reign in life as kings, and they are joint heirs with Jesus Christ. Insecurity and unworthiness are buried in the depths of the sea with their sins when they receive the life and nature of God at their new birth. The competitive edge of Christ secures believers who know who they are in His anointing, and they no longer need to promote themselves. The Bible tells us that all promotion comes from God.

A novice is a person who has not yet matured in Christ, who is still looking for worldly recognition and promotion. This is an open door to jealousy, competition, and strife, which has no place in the ministry, nor in the Body of Christ. This is part of the growth that must occur in order to move an individual from the office of deacon to that of operating in a fivefold ministry gift. Paul told Timothy, his protégé, not to put a novice in an office in the church because that person could get full of pride and conceit, becoming a prey for Satan. Why? A novice is not only one who has insufficient experience, but it is one who still wants others to serve them. They want to get credit for their goody-goody-two-shoes efforts—which is actually dung in the eyes of God. Displays of this nature exemplify a person's character and lack of promotability to serve at another level in the Kingdom of God.

Jesus addressed this same idea in the gospels, when James and John's mother wanted to exalt her sons to sit in positions of honor on Jesus' right and left hand in the Kingdom. The other ten disciples resented this request. None of the twelve had yet acquired the spiritual maturity required for promotion. Jesus told His disciples the qualifications a leader must possess in Matthew 20.

> *And whoever wishes to be first among you shall be your [willing and humble] slave; just as the Son of Man did not come to be served, but to serve, and to give His life as a ransom for many.*
>
> —MATTHEW 20:27–28 AMPC

An elder (bishop or pastor) is one who has spiritually matured enough that he is able to watch over the sheep. He is not concerned about people ministering to his own needs. Love is his aim, not selfishness or self-preoccupation.

Self-Exaltation in Ministry

Over and over in my ministry experience, I have seen the worship leader, due to their high visibility, be overcome with conceit and pride. Lucifer himself, due to his position as the highest archangel in heaven, was another example of a worship leader falling to his own demise and destruction by exalting himself. Remember, visibility in a church does not mean a worship leader is more important than the person who changes the babies' dirty diapers in the nursery. A worship leader who thinks this way might need to trade places with a nursery worker for one Sunday. Whether the worship leader would or not, this is a good gauge of maturity.

I have seen hundreds of believers display self-exaltation and reveal themselves as ministry novices. I once had a couple in my church who were two extremely anointed Bible school graduates. They had functioned well in every area of the ministry of helps in the church. But when I needed them to serve as worship leaders in forefront ministry, it went to their heads.

As the worship leader, the husband assumed he would be given an assigned parking place. None of the staff, including myself as the pastor, had an assigned parking spot. However, one Sunday morning he approached me and said, "Pastor, I have something I want to ask you. Where is my parking place?" I thought, *Dear God, I do not even have a parking place! I just pull in and park anywhere because the Bible says to prefer one another.*

At one time, when my church finally built an office for me, they also marked a parking spot for me with a sign that said *Pastor*. There would be people who would deliberately park in that spot, but I would just park somewhere else. I am too busy doing the work of the ministry to worry about parking spaces. My name on a parking place has nothing to do with my role in ministry.

The second verse of the song "Living in the Presence of Jesus"[10] talks about what is truly important in ministry:

The world can offer flashy deals
And sometimes recognition looks so fine
But titles only go so far
And I've found out a dime ain't worth a dime.
Satan's got one main ambition
Tryin' every way to cut me down
But in Christ I am a winner
And I don't have to get down with that clown.

If you grow up and honor the gift, you will not park in the pastor's space. That is rebellion. The Bible says in 1 Samuel that "rebellion is as the sin of witchcraft" (15:23 KJV). In the meantime, you have touched the anointed. Again, this is another case of self-exaltation, thinking you are more important than the pastor or another church leader.

Let's humble ourselves so we do not get out from under God's divine protection.

That man whom I asked to be my worship leader had come up through the ranks of the ministry of helps. Now that he is in a visible position, he is angry because I did not give him a special parking place. I said, "Brother, I have ten acres here. If you come early, you can park anywhere you want in the parking lot." He did not say anything. He did not even apologize.

This worship leader was not really that stuck up. He and his wife were the sweetest couple I had ever known. They were wonderful people. However, once they moved into the forefront and became visible to the entire congregation, they interpreted it as being in the fivefold ministry.

Do those things happen in the Body of Christ? All the time, yes. People are housed in flesh. Do you know how you get rid of that self-righteous attitude? If you sing and sing and sing, you will sing the parking places away—or whatever other issue your flesh is all bent out of shape over. If you learn to keep your mouth shut, you will not display your immaturity. Then, no one will even know you were in the flesh. Growing up in Christ is a must!

It is so easy to exert ourselves beyond the position or the role we have been given. We must learn how to stay in our rank and not override it. This is a huge lesson in church government and promotion. A sergeant would never override the instructions of a captain in the military, or he would be subject to discipline. We are the army of God, and we must learn to follow the instructions we are given.

The pastor of every local church is submitted to the Lord Jesus Christ, and he must give an account for the local church of which he is the under-shepherd. We all must be submitted to someone. Even Jesus Himself was submitted to His Father God.

The Key to God's Exaltation

If you desire to be used by God at a higher level or in a greater anointing, become an Elisha to an Elijah, or a Joshua to a Moses. This is the fastest road to God's exaltation. Do you know why Elisha was able to perform twice the number of miracles as Elijah did? How did he get that anointing? He did not let Elijah out of his sight. He hung on to him everywhere he went. He was there to do whatever Elijah needed him to do. He never left his side. Wherever Elijah went, there was Elisha. Elijah is a type of Christ; Elisha is a type of the Church.

Did you know there are far more miracles in the Church's history than there were in Jesus' ministry? If you want more from God and you desire to function in a greater way for God, be so available to your pastor that he runs into you everywhere he goes. Be at his side, ready and willing to do whatever he needs done. There is no job too small or too large. You must have an "I-can-do" attitude.

If you want promotion in the Kingdom of God, become so available and faithful to your pastor that he puts you on his staff because you are so valuable. Either that, or he promotes you into your own ministry. It was not until the two prophets passed over the Jordan River that Elijah asked Elisha what he wanted! Only after taking care of Elijah was Elisha qualified to receive what he desired from Elijah (and it actually came from God). His request of Elijah was a double-portion anointing—to be used of God at another level. In order to receive the double anointing like Elijah, death to the self-life and personal ambitions are requirements. Elisha left all for the cause of the Kingdom. This sounds like a hard thing to do, but there is a cost for exaltation.

Exaltation in God's Kingdom will cost you! Submitting yourself under the leadership of a pastor or ministry gift qualifies you. The Bible says that God will exalt you in due time. Most people want a shortcut. You can't be a general in the army of God after a short two-year stint in Bible school. People want to get born again on Monday (the diaper stage) and reach thousands (by being placed in the fivefold ministry) on Friday. There is an apprenticeship with God, just like there is to everything else. So, how intense is your desire to be God's man or God's woman? Are you willing to pay the price?

Chapter Seven

The Importance of Church Structure—Specifically the Roles of Pastor and Worship Leader

And God hath set some in the church, first apostles, secondarily prophets, thirdly teachers, after that miracles, then gifts of healings, helps, governments, diversities of tongues.

—1 CORINTHIANS 12:28 KJV

IN THE LAST CHAPTER, WE DISCUSSED THE FIVEFOLD OFFICES and the ministry of helps in the local church. The worship leader, musicians, and psalmist ministers are all considered supportive roles to the fivefold offices. Everything with God is progressive. He is always looking to develop, groom, and anoint members in the Church to the fullness of His plan for them.

The worship leader is in forefront ministry and is extremely visible. This is a key player to empower a move of God in the Church. It is easy for this person to think their position is a fivefold office. Understanding one's position and place in the Church is key.

Clear communication and guidance between the pastor and worship leader is a must! As I mentioned before, being upfront and visible often causes people who are novices to think more highly of themselves, which causes problems for pastors. In fact, in my experience as a pastor, the three positions that have experienced the greatest turmoil have been the worship leader, the nursery worker, and the intercessor. Most of the problems exist due to the forefront visibility of these positions. It is easy to take on the role of a decision-maker for the pastor when one becomes so noticeable to others in the church.

When every member of the team performs their roles, then Jesus receives the glory and not man. God puts order, structure, and government to everything that He does. If people in their positions violate this order, then the result is confusion or misunderstanding. Staying in your place or position, and fulfilling it with anointing, humility, and respect, brings honor, glory, and praise unto God!

To experience the purest form of worship, there must be a proper relationship between the pastor and the worship leader. Understanding your role, your limits, and your expression as a worship leader or pastor is key to unity, harmony, and anointing. We need to be aware of our position in the Church, and then not violate it.

Too often the pastor does not really understand the critical function of church government and authority. This is where real problems begin. It is easy then for the worship leader to usurp the pastor's role and create confusion on the platform.

Preparation to minister *to God* in worship is the main job of the worship leader. It is not a worship leader's job to cajole and pump the people up to worship God, or even to preach and exhort people to sing. As the leader engages the people in worship and takes them into the inner court, the congregation joins in.

Worship leaders often complain to me about others not entering worship. If you are a worship leader, the way to encourage and sustain worship is for you to get lost in worship to God yourself! You then draw the people into worship through your own heartfelt worship and enthusiasm to God. When people see you are getting excited, raising your hands, opening your mouth, following the instructions of the song, and simply yielding to God, that anointing brings others into the presence of God.

People recognize when worship is not coming from the heart, when it is simply a performance. If you make no attempt at worship, raising your hands, and acting like you are in the mainstream of worship, you hold back others from worship. It should be a mighty stream of praise as your local body is wholly worshiping God together. Worship is unto God, not man!

The Role of the Worship Leader

Music is the best tool in the world to inject life into people. Generally, the worship leader only has about ten to twenty minutes to lead people into worship.

As a worship leader, you must humble yourself and submit to the pastor's leadership. Your place as a worship leader is to minister as John the Baptist did. You are setting the platform for the presentation of the Word and the gift and anointing of the pastor. It is your place to bring a strong atmosphere of victory and anointing into the service through praise and worship. You must be prepared and ready to step into that anointing. Later in this book, I will discuss guidelines and preparations to make you the most effective and anointed in your position.

Many worship leaders try to usurp the pastor's place. If you sing the right songs, Holy Ghost will pour all over him like syrup when he stands up to preach. Everybody in church will then observe the special anointing God has placed on the pastor. This is how you put your pastor over into the anointing.

You are speaking life and praying over your pastor. You have been singing music over him. All he is doing is stepping over into the anointing. You prepare the atmosphere for the Holy Ghost to take His place. God will show you how to minister and what to sing. He will lead you to victorious and triumphant songs describing who you are in Christ to encourage the people and to set the platform for the Word of God.

Building an Atmosphere of Faith and Victory

Here is the chorus of a song that will usher in an atmosphere of victory in a church service. It is entitled "That's What I Have, That's Who I Am":[11]

That's what I have
That's who I am
I am a king come out of Abraham
Because of Christ
I reign in life in Him
That's what I have
That's who I am.

Now, here is another good one, verse one of a song entitled "Our King of Kings":[12]

When life tries to crowd you with doubting
And reason is doubt in disguise
You hold the key to the kingdom
Sing out, and faith will arise.

You say that sounds like a solo? You put that up on the media screen and let the congregation sing those words. The congregation has been out there wallowing in the world all week. They probably sat up until 2 a.m. watching television because it was Saturday night. There is not anything godly on television at two in the morning. There was not much godly on at 5 p.m. either.

The great honor and task of the worship leader is to get the world off the people. Right in the middle of their worries and concerns, you put words of this caliber on the screen and watch God move:

CHORUS:

Kings and priests, He made us to be
We have what we say
We get what we see
Faith is the victory
And love is the key
Jesus is Lord and our King of kings.

People come into a service thinking about their problems in life, like their in-laws, their jobs, and their bosses. Their thoughts might be things like: *I hate my job. I am going to get another job. How am I going to pay my rent this week?*

Then you sing the second verse of that song:

We wrestle not against flesh and blood,
But principalities and powers up high
But the greater One is within me
And He's living big in me now!

These words are powerful to move people from the cares of this life into victory. When the people see these words with the eye gate and sing them with their mouths and spirits, it changes their attitude from fear to faith.

Learning this music is a way of life. Faith is a way of life.

I have just painted a picture with suggested music choices that will create a powerful atmosphere. If this music inspires and encourages the pastor, think what it will do for the people. The pastor has been studying all week, and when he hears the words of that second verse, it lights his fire even further!

The congregation says, "Amen," and they start screaming wild and hopping around. You say, "Does that really happen?" Yes, it really happens. Sometimes in our church we stop in the middle of these songs and flat-out let her go. We praise God for a few minutes, and then we come back and finish the song. Why? The anointing and power of God comes all over the people because Holy Ghost anointing is on the Word of God.

Do you know what is so amazing? As the worship leader, you think *you* picked the songs. However, it was really the Holy Spirit who led you to sing these songs. You may hear comments like, "That service was so profound. Why was our worship so much better this morning?" Maybe you spent an hour praying before you started picking the songs. If you are going to wait until 11 p.m. on Saturday night to prepare for Sunday morning worship, you have already missed it anyway.

The Pastor's Role

If the worship leader does not do his job, then the responsibility falls on the pastor to lead the people into worship. The pastor loses valuable time trying to get the people ready to hear the Word of God that Holy Spirit planned for them through the gift of the pastor.

This is very important! There is only one office that has the right to counsel a Christian, and that is the office of the pastor. That does not mean that a church member has a right to corner the pastor and tie him up for hours and hours behind a closed door, especially if they are an infrequent church attender. Many people want a private consultation, but they refuse to receive the counsel of the pastor on Sunday morning. If believers come to church, God will counsel them. People used to ask me, "Do you counsel people?" Yes, I counsel people every Sunday morning, every Sunday night, and every Wednesday night—through the messages that I preach.

God has many things for pastors to do. God set the local church on the earth so people could understand the Church universal, which is invisible and made up of every individual member of the Body of Christ around the world.

The local church is visible and imprints the Church invisible with the fivefold ministry.

Heaven has as many people up there as there are on the earth. There are a whole lot of people going home. There is a great big table set. Jesus is at the door, wanting to bring His beautiful bride home, the bride over whom He has been speaking faith for more than two thousand years.

God has a system for the local church. He has planned continuity for the believer's life. God gave the Church the gift of the pastor. Believers are supposed to sit under a pastor just like they sat under their moms and dads. God, through that gift, will teach believers from faith to faith and from glory to glory. He will do it line upon line, precept upon precept, here a little, there a little. When believers attend every service, God answers their questions without the pastor even knowing it. The pastor is a supernatural office. We have described a real Spirit-led pastor.

I told my church members that if they came to five straight church services in a row and God did not speak through me to them supernaturally, they are not my sheep. Believers do not have to tell a soul on the earth what they are believing God for or what their needs are. They can just tell God, "Father, I am honoring You. I am submitting myself under the mighty hand of God, the fivefold ministry, which is in this local church. I am obeying You, and

I expect to hear my answer." God will change the sermon just so He can speak to that believer! I have seen Him do it.

I used to tell my congregation, "If God does not speak through me supernaturally, then I will give you five hours behind my door, one hour at a time." I never had to do it when I started sharing this precondition for individual counseling.

As a pastor, if you want to experience a move of God in your church, you are going to have to come on in when the Holy Spirit stirs the water. Worship leaders can only lead people into God's presence. They cannot do it for you, nor can they drive you. The worship leader is an extension of the pastor's hands.

God told me a long time ago that the role of the worship leader is not to prophesy, drive, or preach. They have a John the Baptist ministry. They must usher in the presence of God. As they do, the worship leader decreases so the Word can increase.

Many churches stop in the middle of their worship and take an offering. By following this structure for a church service, the preacher must again work up the congregation afterward for another five minutes. He must exhort the people and get the congregation back in the Spirit. When he does this, he is moving into the mental realm most of the time, and there is no anointing left on him.

However, if the preacher can slide right into his message immediately following a Spirit-led, Word-oriented time of worship, he will be hearing God. If he is sitting right in the middle of the congregation where there are psalms, hymns, and spiritual songs coming forth, watch and see what God does. Believers will be amazed at what they hear from their pastor by the Holy Ghost. This is a Holy Ghost flow. The pastor has already primed the pump through study and prayer and the anointing of God. The result is then *gifts and manifestations of the Holy Ghost.*

Chapter Eight

Psalming to the Lord in Public Worship

O sing unto the LORD *a new song: sing unto the* LORD*, all the earth.*

—PSALM 96:1 KJV

AFTER SETTING A GREAT PLATFORM OF FAITH AND VICTORY through Word-based songs, a congregation is then ready for singing in tongues and psalming or singing new songs to the Lord. Worship leaders, after a strong praise service, step over into the Spirit and have the congregation sing in tongues. This takes your service into another spiritual dimension.

What is "psalming to the Lord"? Psalming is taking words from your spirit and telling God what a great God He is, proclaiming the wonders of who He is. Psalm 96:1 describes this as a "new song" coming straight from your heart to the Lord (KJV). You can also take a known song of praise and sing it back to God. You are exalting and praising Him in the congregation. This takes place when a person comes to minister to God with a new song from the Spirit of God, or an "old" song with which others are familiar.

Psalming is a manifestation of the gift of prophecy, and it prepares the atmosphere in a church service for prophecy to come forth. Prophecy sets the atmosphere for the presentation of the Word. This is not a formula. It is just one way to flow with God. You cannot reduce God to a rule of thumb. Many people in church come up with a formula and say, "This is how to get a move of God." Instead, there are times when people become so tuned in to God, and a strong anointing is so present in the atmosphere, that a prophecy bursts forth without psalming. So, learn to flow with God.

Let's begin by looking at the Word of God exhorting us to psalm to one another:

And being not drunk with wine, wherein is excess; but be filled with the Holy Spirit. Speaking to yourselves in psalms and hymns and spiritual songs, singing and making melody in your heart to the Lord.

—EPHESIANS 5:18–19 KJV

Let the word of Christ dwell in you richly in all wisdom; teaching and admonishing one another in psalms and hymns and spiritual songs, singing with grace in your hearts to the Lord.

—COLOSSIANS 3:16 KJV

O sing unto the LORD a new song: sing unto the LORD, all the earth.

—PSALM 96:1 KJV

I will sing a new song unto thee, O God: upon a psaltery and an instrument of ten strings will I sing praises unto thee.

—PSALM 144:9 KJV

In the Old Testament, God exhorted the people to "sing a new song." Psalm 96 tells us to sing a new song, and in Psalm 144, the people are told to sing and play on guitars or stringed instruments a new song. A psalm is ministry unto the Lord, which is the purpose of spiritual worship in a local church service.

Pastors, do you want to see signs and wonders in your services? Train your worship leaders to flow with God and be sensitive to Him. As I mentioned earlier, it is the job of the worship leader to prepare the atmosphere for the Word of God, as well as a move of the Spirit. The greatest miracles I have ever seen have taken place right in the middle of worship.

In Ephesians 5:19 (as well as in Colossians 3:16), Holy Ghost exhorted the early Church to sing psalms and hymns and spiritual songs. However, before that verse, in Ephesians 5:18, the admonition is given to "be filled with the Spirit" (KJV). One evidence of being filled with the Spirit is praying in tongues. Praying in other tongues gives way to all nine gifts of the Spirit to be made manifest.

We find a listing of these supernatural gifts in 1 Corinthians 12. In one of his books,[13] Dr. Kenneth E. Hagin—a great prophet and teacher who spoke into my life—wrote that praying in the Holy Ghost is the doorway to the supernatural. The apostle Paul in 1 Corinthians 14:15 exhorts us to pray and sing both with our understanding and in the Spirit or in tongues when he says, "I will pray with the spirit, and I will pray with the understanding also: I will sing with the spirit, and I will sing with the understanding also."

Most churches, even Spirit-filled congregations, do not pray or sing in tongues in their public services. Dr. Roy Hicks, a superintendent of the Foursquare denomination for many years, admonished and challenged our Bible school students to sing in tongues in every church service for more than thirty seconds, because most churches never pray or sing in tongues. Or if they do sing in tongues, it is less than thirty seconds or a minute. If you want God's presence in your church service, invite Holy Spirit in through speaking and singing in His language, the language of heaven.

Guidelines for Singing Psalms in a Service

As the worship leader, you have come out of a song in your understanding, and you are ready to sing in tongues. You have built up the congregation with faith and victory to the point that they are ready to explode if you do not release this thing in the Spirit. It is now time to let the Spirit flow through you. It is time to sing in the Spirit, or in tongues.

Do not rush into singing in other tongues. Finish your song purposely. The reason people rush into singing in tongues is because they are insecure. Finish the last song in your understanding and the last word and the last syllable of the song. Do it purposely. You are leading worship, and the flow of the service is under your control. Patiently lead the people into the Spirit. Sing in tongues purposefully and not scattershot. Sing and pronounce every syllable in tongues as you first begin. This will make the transition easy.

As you sing in the Spirit, enter in at the same pitch and timing you were singing the last song in your understanding. For example, when you are coming out of English to sing in the Spirit, and you are singing in the key of F, do not start singing in the key of G or the key of E. Hold the tone and release the Spirit at the same level or pitch as you were singing the last song in your understanding. Enter the Spirit this way so it is a natural thing, not a shock. If you are singing in 4/4 time, do not upbeat it. In other words, in whatever timing and key you were singing the last song, maintain it as you begin singing in tongues.

Remember, Holy Ghost is a real gentleman. He collaborates with you. Do not sing in your understanding in one key and timing and then sing differently in the Spirit, which often happens. When you do this, you are out of sync and harmony with the Spirit, and it brings confusion. People do not know where you are going, and they cannot hook up with what you are leading them to do. Telling people to just "flow with God" or to "sing out to God" is not instruction, nor is it leading them. You must lead them there by personal example. Remember, they are sheep who *require* leadership. Also, do not go back and forth between English and the Spirit. You create confusion by doing that.

When Holy Ghost is leading you to step over into the Spirit, put that microphone up to your mouth and be bold and clear, and lead the congregation in the Spirit. Do not be timid! After singing in tongues, invite people to sing psalms, hymns, and spiritual songs. A little exhortation may be in order initially if this is unfamiliar territory for your congregation, so demonstrate what you mean. Make sure everyone understands what you want done in the church service. Otherwise, you may get a soulish prayer or a cry out to God (emotional response) instead of a psalm to God! Instruct by demonstrating to the people what you mean clearly and simply. If you have an individual who knows how to psalm, encourage them to step in and demonstrate singing a psalm in the congregation.

Psalming and singing new songs to the Lord comes the same way a person receives an utterance for a prophecy. However, remember, a prophecy changes the direction of the service. It is all coming from Holy Ghost. The Spirit of God does not give an individual the whole prophecy, but He gives just a phrase, a thought, or the first few words. You must step out in faith. This is also true in singing a new song or psalming to the Lord. After leading people into singing in tongues, invite people from the congregation to psalm or sing a new song.

Yielding to the Spirit in psalming is just like prophecy. As you close your eyes and listen, Holy Spirit gives you the first few thoughts. Open your mouth and sing that line. As you do, the song of the Lord will come forth out of your mouth just like prophecy. You will flow, and you are ministering unto the Lord. You are speaking to God. You are adoring Him, His Son, His Word, and the attributes of God and His provision given through redemption. This is *not* an expression of how you feel or what is going on in your emotions. It is not anything about you.

When you are singing a song or a psalm in a church service, that is the Holy Spirit in your spirit ministering to the Lord: The flow of the Spirit is from earth to heaven. Prophecy, on the other hand, changes the order of the service and brings the flow of the Spirit from heaven to earth. It is God speaking through you to the congregation.

How does a church service get out of order? When you have an order to things, you do not want a prophecy and then a psalm, and then a psalm, and then a prophecy. Sometimes people sing a prophecy. This is a common experience to both the spiritually learned and unlearned. Singing a prophecy does not make it a psalm just by singing it. A prophecy changes the order of the service from heaven to earth instead of earth to heaven. As a result, the pastor or leader must redirect the service accordingly.

Over and over, I have seen a person start with a spiritual psalm/song. They were singing to God, and the flow was from earth to heaven. Someone then follows with a tongue and an interpretation, and by putting a tune with it, thinks it is a psalm. It is not out of order as such. It was edifying, exhorting, and comforting. It was in order that way, but it literally changed the direction and flow of the Spirit as they brought forth a prophecy in music. It changed the flow of the Spirit. Just putting a tune to it does not make it a psalm or a song; you still brought forth a prophecy. God can sing, so do not make a U-turn in the Spirit.

When an individual in the congregation changes the order of service, it is important as a leader to clarify and direct the service appropriately. By explaining to the congregation what is happening in the Spirit, the people will learn. This is not being critical. The more accurate we are in the Spirit with the direction (earth-to-heaven and heaven-to-earth) of the service, the purer the atmosphere is for God to manifest Himself.

Learn to relax in God's presence. Do you want to know how you relax when you are in front of people? Pray in the Holy Ghost. Praying in the Holy Ghost does not give you faith. Praying in the Holy Ghost gives you a capacity in your spirit to direct or aim your faith. Jude 20 uses the phrase, "Building up yourselves on your most holy faith" (KJV). If you are a pastor, get prepared in your spirit before you get in the pulpit and you will flow. God will speak to you. It will be so natural that you will doubt the supernatural. The manifestation of the supernatural is what makes it look natural. Otherwise, it looks like a performance.

Chapter Nine

The Lifestyle of a Worship Leader

Humble yourselves in the sight of the Lord, and he shall lift you up.

—JAMES 4:10 KJV

PREPARATION FOR LEADING WORSHIP IN A CHURCH SERVICE is more than just picking out three or four songs and communicating those songs to the worship team. The worship leader's lifestyle plays a major role in the preparation for leading worship and being effective.

Sensitivity to the Holy Spirit and learning to flow with Him does not happen outside of the preparation of your spirit. Before getting on a platform, you must have spent time in the presence of God *by yourself.*

Holy Spirit told me a vital truth years ago regarding prayer and praise. All the universe is held together by energy, the highest form of energy is prayer—and the highest form of prayer is praise. Everything in the universe is held together by it.

Getting before God and singing faith and ministering to the Lord is profound. It is your place as the worship leader to be in an atmosphere and attitude of praise and worship when you step on the platform.

This preparation does not begin Saturday night at 11:00 p.m. This preparation is what happens in your everyday life. I have often said on the radio that if you lie down with dogs, you get up with fleas. This is a carnal expression, but it depicts the results of any negative relationships in which you may find yourself. Your associations affect you positively or negatively. By hanging around the devil or those who feed their flesh more than their spirit, it will rub off on you and display itself on stage. No life of God will come out of you when the world infiltrates you and your mind.

In the spiritual arena, it is the same thing. When you minister, your preparation (or lack of it) is on full display. When you get ready to go to the platform, make sure you have total control of yourself. Remember, the Holy Spirit collaborates with you. God called you to put the pastor before the people so he can present the Word. God calls and exalts you, but first you must submit to Him. Jesus Christ came from the glory of heaven and submitted Himself in this earth, yet God exalted Him.

> *Let this mind be in you, which was also in Christ Jesus: Who, being in the form of God, thought it not robbery to be equal with God: But made himself of no reputation, and took upon him the form of a servant, and was made in the likeness of men: And being found in fashion as a man, he humbled himself, and became obedient unto death, even the death of the cross. Wherefore God also hath highly exalted him, and given him a name which is above every name: That at the name of Jesus every knee should bow, of things in heaven, and things in earth, and things under the earth; and that every tongue should confess that Jesus Christ is Lord, to the glory of God the Father.*
>
> —PHILIPPIANS 2:5–11 KJV

If Jesus submitted Himself to the Father God, you and I can do no less. Believers submit themselves to Jesus Christ as the One whom God has placed in all authority over heaven, earth, and hell.

When God puts you in a position, and the anointing of God is on you, step into that place with a boldness like a lion. Understand that you are a part of the tribe of Judah. As a minister *of* the Lord and a minister *unto* the Lord, you must have confidence in the position God has given you. You must believe and have confidence in yourself.

I have heard people say that I was confident or bold. Absolutely! The only thing that makes someone bashful or intimidated is not being sure of a subject or being unprepared in spirit. When you are prepared to do anything for God, you are chomping at the bit to get in that pulpit to minister. When you have something to minister and you know it, you are ready, set, go. You are ready to minister *to* God and *for* God.

As the worship leader, you must be prepared to make the worship good, strong, and powerful. It is your ministry assignment to make people conscious of God in preparation for the presentation of the Word. Rehearsing God's presence in your personal life is the best preparation for leading others into worship.

Until you become God-inside conscious, you live a sense-ruled life. Once you come to the full revelation of who you are in Christ and who Christ is in you, everything changes. You quit running around with some of the crowd of people with whom you used to associate and fellowship. You guard your words, your friends, and what you hear. Jesus does not like gossip, and the Spirit of God lives inside you. When you become conscious of Him, you live a more separated life.

It is the place of worship leaders to bring the people into the presence of God and make them God-inside conscious. You cannot take people to a place where you have not been. Through your music and song choices, you make people God-inside conscious.

We are living in the New Covenant with new instructions and blessings in which we live, move, and have our being. We are to live out of the epistles written in the New Testament. However, the Church has learned very few songs based on the letters written to the Church. Much of our reading, teaching, and singing should be grounded in the epistles. Why? These are the specific books of the Bible that the Holy Spirit has given to the Church for this dispensation.

Few songwriters have written music directly from the epistles. Obviously, to write about being a new creature in Christ and the in-Him realities, you must know these truths. David Ingles is one of the modern-day songwriters who has purposely written on the redemptive realities in Christ. It has been his calling to write faith-based music.

Prior to leading worship, you should have acted out the whole service in your living room sometime that week. You should have gotten before the Lord and ministered unto Him. If you do this, just watch what Holy Ghost will do through you. He will put the exact songs in your heart that will prepare the people for the message by the pastor. You will be in sync with your pastor because you heard from heaven, too. You will get up Sunday morning and surprise the pastor because you already outlined his message in music. Where do you think the pastor is getting his message? The pastor may have thought it was just his good thoughts. No, it was Holy Ghost! Where are you going to get your anointing? Holy Ghost! You are both making the atmosphere ready for God to move in the lives of the people. Mission accomplished!

24/7 Calling

> *And the yoke (burden) shall be destroyed because of the anointing.*
>
> —Isaiah 10:27 KJV

> *How God anointed Jesus of Nazareth with the Holy Ghost and with power: who went about doing good,*

> *and healing all that were oppressed of the devil; for God was with him.*
>
> —ACTS 10:38 KJV

A man or woman of God, as well as every worship leader, teacher, and supporting minister in the Church, must separate himself from the world. I am going to make a bold statement: If God placed you in the ministry as a worship leader, it is a twenty-four-hour-a-day calling. Most ministers do not take their calling seriously unless they are in a fivefold office. The anointing does not come on you only when you are going to church.

God calls deacons, and He places gifts in the Body of Christ. It is not men (or Mama) who calls people into the ministry. God does! God always exalts faithful people. The calling of the worship leader in the Body of Christ necessitates a set-apart or separated life.

The entire church will be watching you! When you become the worship leader, you live in a glass house. Everybody knows every little dumb thing your kid does, and everybody talks about it, too. You are front and center—completely visible. You must lean on Him, "casting all your care upon Him; for he careth for you" (1 Pet. 5:7 KJV). In this text, the Holy Spirit is talking to the people working in the Church, telling them to cast their care over on Him. Go read it. The "care" He is talking about is the backbiting of other people against you and against the call of God on you. If you are in the ministry, you know what I am talking about.

As a worship leader, discipline yourself under the Spirit of God and do not override your pastor's office. With the exaltation of being in the forefront ministry, keep a humble spirit about you. Know your place and do not override it. Read the fourth and fifth chapters of First Peter with these thoughts in mind.

Most of the problems in the church result from competition. Competition brings strife, so do not get into competition with other people. Fill your position and do it as unto God. You would be surprised how good worship is when there is unity without strife.

Listen to me, pastors: You do not need someone with a music degree to lead worship. You just need someone who understands spiritual things. Do not put a novice into that position. It will create havoc in the local church.

The very first time I stood before a congregation and told them I was a psalmist, I felt like a liar. However, God told me to step forward and proclaim my ministry. A psalmist is not an office; it is a ministry. As I stood there, I experienced a barrage of negative thoughts, such as: *I wish I had prayed longer and prepared more.* As I was singing, people were falling under the power of the Spirit. But I was so tired, and I kept thinking about myself and how awful it was. God had something to say about it by His Spirit.

There was a woman in the congregation who kept looking at me. The Spirit of God kept drawing me to her. Finally, I realized God wanted to speak a word to me through her.

I stopped and said, "Sister, would you give us what the Lord said?"

She said, "Well, Brother Jerry, it is kind of personal."

I said, "Is it for me?"

She said, "Yes, but it is personal."

I said, "I have never done anything in my life that I am ashamed of. If I need correction, so does the rest of this congregation. Speak it out."

In my mind, I was judging what the Holy Spirit was doing through me.

Through her, the Spirit of God said, "Son, don't strive for excellence and don't strive for quality. You're anointed of Me. That's excellence! That's quality! That's Me!"

There I was, striving for some standard I had set in my head and thinking I was doing so poorly. All the while, God was moving mightily despite my ignorance.

The entire prophetic word was this:

> *Don't strive for excellence. Don't strive for quality. You're anointed of Me. That's excellence! That's quality! That's Me! When you step from this place behind this sacred desk, and you stand at the back door, and someone comes up after the service and tells you how great the service was, don't you judge what comes out of your mouth under My anointing or you will bind My hand to judge it. Don't steal My glory. Just say, "It's good to be a Christian."*

How does that fit into the psalmist ministry and the leading of worship? It fits perfectly. These are the things that put worship leaders over. Do not be ashamed of your position. It is one of the most vital roles in the Church. It is your job to take the people into the throne room, and it is your place to do it. Confidence in God's ability to flow through you, and your confidence in yourself to hear God speak to you and through you, are necessary to accomplish your calling.

Sensitivity to the Holy Spirit

When the worship leader has the anointing of God and is sensitive to the direction of the Holy Spirit, a great refreshing comes upon the people of God during worship. At this point, the people's hearts commune with God. However, if the leader is insensitive to the moving of the Holy Spirit, there is an obvious missing the mark. This lack of agreement with the ministry of the Word and Holy Ghost makes it difficult for the Word to come forth. When the people's hearts are not prepared to hear the Word through meaningful praise and worship, Holy Ghost does not accomplish everything He desires. Therefore, the importance of unity between the worship leader and the rest of the ministry team, especially the pastor, is vital. An effective worship leader will be sensitive to the pastor and the direction God is giving to him. This promotes unity:

> *Behold, how good and how pleasant it is for brethren to dwell together in unity! It is like the precious ointment upon the head, that ran down upon the beard, even Aaron's beard: that went down to the skirts of his garments.*
>
> —Psalm 133:1–2 KJV

We see in Psalm 133 that unity and anointing are co-dependent upon each other. Signs, wonders, and miracles come when God's people are in unity. Throughout the Scriptures, we see the great things God does when the people of God come together as one in the Spirit.

One major New Testament example of unity is in the upper room where the disciples were praying and waiting on God on the Day of Pentecost, as recorded in Acts 2. Several days later, they were praying, and the Holy Ghost moved once again.

> *And when they had prayed, the place was shaken where they were assembled together; and they were all filled with the Holy Ghost, and they spake the word of God with boldness. And the multitude of them that believed were of one heart and of one soul: neither said any of them that ought of the things which he possessed was his own; but they had all things common.*
>
> —ACTS 4:31–32

These are just two examples of the power of unity and the blessings that come from unity in the Spirit.

Remember, you cannot get a move of God if you are not singing the Word of God. Worship begins by praising God and edifying those around you. As you flow with God, the atmosphere keeps building and building.

If you do this, the congregation will walk into the church, and within two or three minutes, they will be flowing in the gifts of the Spirit. They will shake the world off. This becomes a way of life. Worship is not just something we do when we go to church. We get into ruts by thinking that worship and prayer are expressions that happen in a designated sequence of time.

One song, "In the Chamber,"[14] explains how we worship our way into His presence:

Father, I worship You
Out of my spirit
Blessing and thanking You
In our own way
Your heart I covet
Lord, Your will and purpose
Into submission I surrender this day.

Chorus:

Into the chamber
Be free, Holy Spirit,
Speak through me gently
As I close the door
    Heavenly Lover
    Let Thy presence cover
    Shekinah unending
    Is all I long for.

You get over there in the Spirit. As you do, you position yourself and open the floodgates so God can minister back to you. When you get into the chamber and submit yourself—any wife knows this—she gets blessed. You see, the song says, "Heavenly Lover, let Thy presence cover, Shekinah unending."

We want the manifest presence and glory of God.

Anointing and Professionalism

Professionalism denotes music skill and knowledge, neat clothes, a sharp appearance, and managing oneself with poise and confidence. Professionalism is something a person naturally portrays in preparation for ministry.

On the other hand, anointing comes through personal preparation in the Spirit and the Word of God. It is the outworking of the Holy Ghost. The anointing comes from God.

Professionalism and anointing are not the same thing. One is man-ward, and the other is God-ward. If you blend them together, you have a dynamic duo! Many people try to replace the anointing with professionalism. Professionalism alone will not bring God's Spirit into the atmosphere. The heart of God needs to be present. Knowledge and information alone puff up.

If you take your preparation and study built around God's Word, you have a good foundation. Be faithful and consistent. Be humble and submit yourself to God. You see, faithfulness causes the anointing. Be faithful to God.

Be faithful to your pastor. Be faithful to your church. Be faithful to the position in which God has placed you, and you will walk in the anointing. When you step up to minister, the overflow of the anointing causes the blind to see, the deaf to hear, and the lame to walk.

Just like the world, the church often places the young, pretty, and talented ones on stage. However, every now and then, some little gal in a hand-me-down dress and an old guitar starts singing, and the power of God drops in the place. Everyone falls to the floor weeping because of the presence of God. The anointing of God is always on the Word!

There is nothing wrong with either anointing or professionalism. By blending them, you have a dynamic duo. Anointing does not always have feeling. Anointing does not always have a college degree. Anointing does not always have the proper grammar. Anointing is not the perfect weight and the perfect height. A sense-ruled man thinks these are mandatory characteristics. You want the polish, shine, and excellence, but not at the expense of the anointing.

Saul was afraid to be king of Israel, so he hid among the baggage. They had to search for him when the prophet wanted to anoint him. Even when Saul got into sin, he offered a sacrifice instead of obeying God.

In doing so, he lost his anointing and kingship. God had already sent Samuel the prophet to anoint David to become the next king.

Little old, ruddy David—even in his youth—knew enough to keep his mouth off the anointed one. When David located Saul in the cave and cut off Saul's coattail, it grieved him in his heart. Have you ever talked about your pastor and felt bad about it? This is what happened to David.

God had already looked over the edge of heaven at David right in the middle of the sheep while he was singing, "Bless the Lord, O my soul." And God said, "I have made Me a king." God will also make and manifest all that He wants out of you through the praise and worship you offer to Him.

You see, your music *is* you! Study it in the Bible. Praise and worship *is* you! It is how you represent God: "[God] will hasten [His] word to perform it" (Jer. 1:12 KJV).

Third John 2 says, "Beloved, I wish above all things that thou mayest prosper and be in health, even as thy soul prospereth" (KJV). Until you get your mind renewed to think prosperous thoughts, you will be poor. Until you get your mind renewed enough by hearing the Word of God to where you truly believe that "by [His] stripes ye were healed" (1 Pet. 2:24 KJV), you will be sick. However, when you eat it, sleep it, think it, and dream it, then healing just happens. You will not need oil, prayer cloths, anointing, binding and loosing, or a prayer of agreement. It will just happen.

God's best is for you to stay under the *chuppah* and stay in perfect health. Remember the Jewish song in which the wedding couple stood under the *chuppah* (canopy) in *Fiddler on the Roof*? The canopy the couple stood under represented the divine protection and provision of God over their marriage. If you stay in fellowship and in love with each other, it will keep the *chuppah*, or protection, over your marriage. If they got a hole in the *chuppah*, they lost their blessings. The *chuppah* is a natural type of a spiritual reality.

If you run off your mouth against someone and you do not sing and praise God, you will get a hole in your *chuppah*, and soon the circumstances of life move right in. Poverty rolls right in. Sickness rolls right in. You see, healing is one thing. Divine health is far better. First John 1:9 keeps you protected under the *chuppah* of God: "If we confess our sins, he is faithful and just to forgive us our sins, and to cleanse us from all unrighteousness" (KJV).

Chapter Ten

Priming the Pump to Worship in the Spirit

For as many as are led by the Spirit of God, they are the sons of God.

—Romans 8:14 KJV

There are three things that must happen in a church service. The people must: 1) feel good about themselves; 2) feel good about each other; and 3) feel good about God. If you have all three of these things in a service, you have had good church.

As the worship leader, it is your job to make people feel good about themselves. Always remember, your focus and goal must be to set the platform for the Word to come forth. The main goal of the church service is to minister to the people.

God designates direction and purpose for every kind of service. There are: 1) believers' meetings; 2) evangelistic thrusts; 3) teaching or seminars; and 4) healing meetings, to name a few. Regular Sunday morning services have a different purpose from an evangelistic meeting. Knowing the purpose of each service guides you into the proper and meaningful order of service to fulfill the intent of each meeting.

The concepts and principles regarding worship leading related in this book are primarily instructions and guidance to worship leaders who are leading worship on a Sunday morning service in a local body of believers. These guidelines resulted from a lifetime of ministry experience in both church and field ministry.

Remember, your goal as a worship leader is to present an atmosphere of faith and victory so that the Word can come forth in truth and reality. As discussed previously regarding the lifestyle of a worship leader, we talked about the value of your personal ministry to God and hearing from Him. You have been on your knees before the Lord, and you have heard from heaven. As you minister throughout the week to the Lord, God speaks and reveals the songs and music for the upcoming service.

Every night, I place a pencil and paper by a lamp next to my bed. This way, when God awakens or speaks to me in the night, I will be ready to write down what He is saying. Oftentimes, the Holy Spirit does not speak to us in the day because we are so busy. The Lord must almost shut us down long enough so He can speak.

God is speaking all the time. Jesus, in teaching a parable of the Kingdom, said, "And the cares of this world, and the deceitfulness of riches, and the lusts of other things entering in, choke the word, and it becometh unfruitful" (Mark. 4:19 KJV). These are the things coming against you to stop you from hearing from God.

When you go to bed at night, your mind and body shut down—but your spirit never sleeps. God is a Spirit, and He never sleeps. On the other hand, your body shuts down so your spirit can pick up on what God is speaking. Before you know it, you might even think it is a dream or you might have a word from the Lord. You now have direction in life or ministry.

The best sermons I ever preached came together in a similar manner. I would be thinking I was going to preach a certain message, and God would wake me up in the middle of the night and change what I was going to preach. I would tell him how many hours I had already studied in preparation. He would simply say that study was just for me. The Bible says in 2 Timothy 2:15, "Study to shew thyself approved unto God, a workman that needeth not to be ashamed, rightly dividing the word of truth" (KJV).

As I mentioned, you must get prepared in your spirit to minister to God. This is how you lead people into worship. As a result of the preparation of your spirit and overflow from being in God's presence, the crowd gets the overflow of your ministry to God.

I strongly recommend that you discipline yourself to listen to faith music. If you are going to embrace the message of faith, you ought to embrace the music of faith. Guard it with your heart. Do not get up there and sing garbage. Keep the music to New Covenant worship.

You were born again at the new birth. You want Spirit-led worship. You do not need to clap, shout, holler, and all of that to turn on a crowd. If you get something anointed, Holy Spirit will be there. You do not have to sing some little ditty to make the Holy Spirit get on people. Sing the anointing! Sing the Word! Sing about Jesus!

Pick out your music. Go through your music. Make sure it says something good about God. Sing songs that make people feel good about each other and about themselves.

Get people's mind on the fact that Jesus is their answer, not their problem, with songs like "El Shaddai (You're Such a Good God to Me)."[15] The chorus goes like this:

Almighty Father, El Shaddai
You pour Your life into me
Nourishment, Provider, Strength Giver, Satisfier
You're such a good God to me.

Singing Songs with Understanding and Revelation

Many times, in church circles, we become so engrossed in our problems that we miss the revelation and understanding of what God is saying to us. For example, Holy Spirit will use a song to direct our spirits and to lead us into the path of victory—if we have ears to hear.

I was in the airport at Guatemala City, Guatemala, with a mission team of twenty missionaries and other ministry leaders. Our mission involved traveling on a volcano spewing lava, and the objective was to minister at an Indian village. Along with the erupting volcano, no one in our group could speak Spanish. These challenges generated much fear in the group. One challenge alone would have been enough! But then, the group began singing a well-known song called "Great Is the Lord":

Great is the Lord
And greatly to be praised
In the city of our God
In the mountain of his holiness
Beautiful for situation
The joy of the whole earth
Is Mount Zion on the side of the north
The city of the great King.

We were singing God's response to our griping and complaining without realizing it. God *is* beautiful for situation! A prophecy came forth after singing this song. The Lord said, "Didn't I hear you say that I am beautiful for situations? Stop rehearsing the problem. I have the problem in hand. Just worship Me!"

On another occasion, I was in a church where a group of people were praying about a move of God. They were praying and asking God for a manifestation of the power of God and for signs and wonders. However, they were praying in unbelief. For eight solid months, they kept singing a song, "The Joy of the Lord," every time they gathered for prayer, and they did not see the reality of what God was saying. He was leading them and providing instruction, but they did not hear or see the answer:

The word of faith is nigh thee
even in thy mouth
The word of faith is nigh thee
even in thy mouth
The word of faith is nigh thee
even in thy mouth.
The joy of the Lord is my strength.[16]

They were singing the answer found in Romans 10:8, but they did not recognize it. God was telling them, "You have the word of faith, and the answer is in your mouth. Now, act on it!" The apostle James exclaims in James 2:17, "Faith, if it hath not works, is dead" (KJV). Romans 10:8 puts it this way: "But what saith it? The word is nigh thee, even in thy mouth, and in thy heart: that is, the word of faith, which we preach" (KJV).

Chapter Eleven

Ministering from the Overflow of God

If any man thirst, let him come unto me, and drink. He that believeth on me, as the scripture hath said, out of his belly shall flow rivers of living water.

—John 7:37–38 KJV

When I first became acquainted with the message of faith, I started searching for music other than the unbelieving songs about people's earth-walk that so many Christians sing. People are always singing about their great, future life in heaven, or crying out to God to fix their problems. Generally, there is no singing of the past-tense Gospel confession of the finished work of Christ and their faith in it or of the Pauline revelation. I needed new music to complement the word of faith I was preaching. Jesus has completed His work. Christ finished the work of redemption with His death and resurrection. We are partakers of the completed work in Him. We are joint heirs and heirs of God. Greater is He that is in us (2 Pet. 1:4; Rom. 8:17; 1 John 4:4).

While visiting the mission field in Guatemala, God spoke to me for eight days, giving me instruction about my ministry. One of the things He told me was that I would begin to sing new songs. The new songs I was to sing by the Spirit of God were primarily David Ingles' music. It was the music of the new creation—the in-Him realities—that corresponded with the Pauline epistles. Essentially, this meant the past-tense Gospel. As I mentioned, the work of Christ is done, completed, finished!

When I first started a church as the home base for our mission work in Guatemala, I called it Living Water Teaching Church. In the beginning, we would have two solid hours of worship singing new-creation music. After the worship, I would follow the Holy Ghost and obey His instructions.

In those days, I watched the Spirit of God fall, and the people would kneel behind the pews because the presence of God was so strong. There would be wave after wave after wave of God's power that would pass through the sanctuary and touch everybody! Everyone would get healed! Teeth would grow. Blind eyes would see. That is the power of praise when we sing about Him, and when we sing about the name of Jesus and His power!

God wills this in your praise and worship. The problem is, we never get to this place of pure praise and worship. Most often, worship becomes a form of godliness denying the power thereof. Your worship will never be any more powerful than the songs you are singing. You cannot sing about the little brown church in the dale and how you feel—all the while rehearsing your problems in your mind—and just make everyone cry. That kind of worship does not heal anyone. I can sing songs about Mama and make you cry. I know a lot of them. I have written half a dozen songs about Mom. It is all right on Mother's Day for a special. However, I never did see anyone receive healing while singing about Mom. We want to sing about the glory of Jesus. He is the Savior, Healer, Deliverer, and mighty Provider!

Did you ever get in front of a church and sing the first song, and the place explodes in praise, and you insist that the Word is going to burst inside of you? The worship leader stands up and sings in the Spirit, and things further explode. You do not have to sing three songs. If you are a worship leader and you sense a strong presence of God, stop right there and follow the Holy Spirit. God will direct you in what to do.

Worship leaders tell me all the time they must sing songs about where the people in the congregation are emotionally and what is going on with them in their heads. Says who? Where does the Bible tell us to sing songs about our emotions and feelings? Set the standard. Do not follow the popular ideas of worship.

If you preach the Word and sing "Yankee Doodle," there is no continuity in the Spirit. In fact, you cause confusion in people's spirits. By singing about the new creation and who you are in Christ, you bring people over into the Spirit realm.

To get a consistent move of the Spirit, you must have a continuity of the Spirit. God will work with what you have, but God's Spirit will fill the room with His presence when you sing the Word. Remember, the anointing does not always have feelings.

To be sensitive to Holy Spirit publicly, you must be sensitive in the prayer closet. People always want to hurry the Holy Ghost and try to get Him to move by giving people goose bumps. If you move by the Word of God, Holy Ghost moves automatically.

God has sent me all over America singing new-creation music. Many churches fought me over it. I laughed and sang music about who believers are in Christ. I gave birth to hope and faith in the hearts of people through this music in preparation to receive a miracle from God. Also, if you sing music from the epistles, your church government remains accurate and balanced according to the Word of God.

Everything done in ministry should be out of your overflow of God. Teach from your overflow. Lead worship from your overflow. Pray from your overflow. Write from your overflow. To get the Holy Ghost involved, do all your ministry from your overflow. In other words, pray in tongues and stay full of the Word, and Holy Spirit will do the rest!

Chapter Twelve

Worship Leader Guidelines

Moreover, it is required in stewards, that a man be found faithful.

—1 CORINTHIANS 4:2 KJV

IN THIS CHAPTER, I WANT TO LOOK AT GUIDELINES FOR A worship leader. These guidelines result from my lifetime of ministry as a worship leader, psalmist, pastor, and teacher. In earlier chapters, we addressed some of these guidelines, but they bear repetition here.

1. Follow Instructions.

First, do not go beyond your pastor's directions and instruction. If the pastor has said he wants the worship to last for ten minutes, do not go twelve minutes. No excuses. The spirit is in subjection to the prophet (1 Cor. 14:32).

On one occasion, Dr. Kenneth E. Hagin invited me to minister with him in a meeting in Oklahoma City, where he was conducting a Holy Ghost seminar. He wanted me to minister prior to his teaching like I do on the radio. He explained that the psalmist ministry is part of the equipping of the office of the prophet.

He shared in the service that he would change his teaching to his students after hearing me minister on the radio prior to his 11:00 a.m. class at Rhema Bible Training Center. During the Oklahoma City meeting, he instructed me to minister with my guitar for ten minutes. I did not go eleven minutes. I did exactly what the prophet had instructed me to do. In his meetings at Rhema, he would tell singers to sit down if they sang songs that did not equip him to operate in the office of the prophet. I was obedient to his time limit and instructions!

As mentioned before, the pastor is the final authority in the local church. The buck stops with him. He is the one responsible to God for everything that happens in that church and its services. Do not violate him. To bring continuity, unity, and harmony, learn to flow with him and obey his guidance.

2. Exhibit Faithfulness and Confidence.

The Bible tells us, "Moreover it is required in stewards, that a man be found faithful" (1 Cor. 4:2 KJV). Your faithfulness to your man of God is the level of your faithfulness to God. Be faithful to your pastor, his leadership, and your church. And most importantly, be faithful to God.

Trust and confidence are invaluable if you are to operate at the highest possible level in God's calling on your life. Have confidence in God and in your pastor. Most importantly, have confidence in yourself as you stand before the people and lead them into becoming God-conscious through worship.

Another word the Bible uses for *confidence* is "boldness"; that is, spiritual boldness. It takes boldness and courage to step into the anointing in which God and your pastor expect you to stand. Without boldness, you might not step out and follow the Holy Ghost when He is moving. It takes faith to be bold and confident in the position and calling of God as Spirit-filled men and women of God.

3. Be Humble (1 Pet. 5:6; James 4:10).

Along with boldness, confidence, and faithfulness must come humility. Boldness and confidence are spiritual characteristics. Knowing how to yield your privileges—when to increase and decrease in ministry—is critical as a worship leader. Remember, self-exaltation stinks in the nostrils of God! The Bible tells us that pride—including grumbling in a ministry position—comes before a fall. Satan is the king of pride. You are there to lift the hands of your pastor and put him over. Do not forget that all ministry is unto God first and primarily!

4. Be Prepared in Your Spirit.

Make worship good, strong, and powerful. You are setting the platform for the Word of God. For this strong worship to occur, you must be prepared in your spirit. Preparation is a way of life. Prepare by ministering to the Lord throughout the week—and especially prior to the time of ministry.

5. Stay in Your Position.

Many worship leaders do an injustice to the pastor or ministry leader by preaching between every song. It is not your job to exhort, encourage, and preach to the congregation. Urging them to worship God is unnecessary and an indication that you are not fulfilling your position. You are not the pastor, preacher, or teacher. I often see this habit of preaching between songs as commonplace in charismatic circles; however, it overrides the pastor's authority. As the worship leader, you must usher in the presence of God. It is a John-the-Baptist ministry; you must decrease so the Word of God can increase.

6. Picking Out Songs, Chords, and Keys.

In preparing your song selection, maintain a steady tempo. Do not jump, for example, from a song in 2/4 time to 4/4 time in the music selection. Make the song selection flow easily and naturally from one song and key to another.

Many times, worship leaders sing their songs in a lower key, making it more difficult for the congregation to sing with them. I always tell my worship team to make the people work for the songs by singing in a higher key. Also sing songs to God out of your belly, not your head, to maximize your worship to the Lord.

Song selection for Sunday morning should be familiar songs to the congregation. For the launch of a new song on Sunday morning, sing it as a special with the words on the media screen to provide an initiation to the words. Always charge Sunday morning with energy and life to enable the congregation to worship God freely and out of their hearts. It is much more difficult to worship God with new or unknown words and music. No matter how much you cajole people to sing, a new song does not optimize the greatest worship to God. This is especially true if you want a move of God in your church on a Sunday morning.

7. Train the People to Sing to the Lord.

In an earlier chapter, we talked about teaching and encouraging people to psalm and sing songs unto the Lord. As a worship leader, you must demonstrate singing a psalm; that is, show them by example how to do it. Sing your music with expression, singing out the song with passion like you believe it, not like you are romancing your wife or in some ho-hum fashion. Even the greatest song with the most powerful words of faith, if half-heartedly sung, will not produce results.

8. Always Maintain Professionalism on the Platform.

Worship leaders sometimes try to direct other members of the worship team or sound team while they are singing. This is unprofessional. The congregation sees every move of the worship team, including their facial expressions, their talking to other members of the worship team, or any hand gestures or signals. Anything obviously done outside of your worship shows a lack of professional behavior. If communication needs to happen, be as discreet as possible.

I always instructed my worship leaders that if something happens that is funny or challenging on stage, do not show it on your face. Act like everything is perfect. Keep the entire congregation thinking everything is as expected, even if something goes awry.

Above all, do not show on your face any problems or frustrations. Everyone sees every facial expression you and the worship team make. While you are on stage, everyone is watching everything that is visible from the platform. Your actions can be distracting to the congregation.

9. Be in Sync and in Harmony with Your Pastor.

Great worship leaders must understand church etiquette, its operation, and especially God's character. This topic could fill a seminar. Many of these guidelines involve the character of God and the fruit of the Spirit. Remember, you are representing God and your pastor while leading people in worship.

10. Lead the People in Worship; Do Not Drive Them.

Remember, the worship team has often been practicing and in worship for several hours before the people even enter the church. Do not try to get the congregation to where you are in a few minutes. Do not push them. You must lead them by example.

You are ministering to God, not the people. You lead people in worship by acting like you and God are the only ones in the room. By immersing yourself in worship to God as you sing songs of faith and victory, the people will follow you right into the presence of God. As you move into the Spirit, you bring the people to where you are in the Spirit, and God can move in and among the people.

11. Consider When to Give the Announcements.

The church service should be a smooth flow. There should be a continuity in the Spirit from start to finish, with one continuous message or theme. In most churches, we bring a good presence of God into the service—and then we turn around and immediately take an offering. We could experience a greater move of God if we made the announcements at the end of the service or determine another means of communication with the congregation, such as a bulletin, church website, or media slide. We need to experience a move of God with our worship, and then we should move right away into the presentation of the Word of God.

Our habits need to change if ministry is our goal. By taking the offering or giving the announcements right after the worship, we lose the momentum the Holy Spirit is bringing so He can accomplish His purpose. These could follow the conclusion of the service, and that would allow for a greater move of God.

12. Set a Standard.

"Blessed are those who hunger and thirst for righteousness, for they will be filled" (Matt. 5:6 NIV). If you are a worship leader, it is your job to create an atmosphere of hunger. You are God's champion standing there. You are supposed to look like Jesus, smell like Jesus, and talk like Jesus. This is the Gospel truth—you should be a walking, living, and breathing epistle. The Bible is not the spoken Word; it is the *logos* until the Word is in you. The Word that sets you free is the Word that you know and act upon. There is a big difference. You can lay the Word down on your mantle and still miss heaven because you never put the Word of God in you. By meditating day and night according to Joshua 1:8, you will make your way prosperous, and you will have great success.

Experiencing spiritual worship in a church service is integral to the moving of the Spirit and to impacting the lives of the people of God. To experience a greater move, we must function and flow in the realm of the Spirit, not from our flesh.

> *In the last day, that great day of the feast, Jesus stood and cried, saying, If any man thirst let him come unto me, and drink. He that believeth on me, as the scripture hath said, out of his belly shall flow rivers of living water. (But this spake he of the Spirit, which they that believe on him should receive: for the Holy Ghost was not yet given; because that Jesus was not yet glorified.)*
>
> —JOHN 7:37–39 KJV

Chapter Thirteen

Schooling People into Faith Through Worship

Meditate upon these things; give thyself wholly to them; that thy profiting may appear to all.

—1 TIMOTHY 4:15 KJV

AS BELIEVERS, WE HAVE A GLORIOUS INHERITANCE IN JESUS Christ. Yet, to listen to most Christians, it sounds as though the devil has the upper hand instead of God. I often say that people need a daily refilling with the Word of God, as the *Zoe*-life of God leaks out as they brush up against people in their daily walks of life. Most preachers who preach and teach faith still do not sing predominately faith songs in their services. We lose a mighty, powerful component to discipling and bringing our churches and individuals into the fullness of God when we are not purposeful in our worship. To prepare and excel the presence of God as worship leaders, sing songs of faith that reinforce righteousness, redemption, and the new creation. This will propel you to your primary objective.

Many songwriters do not have the revelation of who they are in Christ, and they have not majored on the new-creation realities. David Ingles is truly an apostle of new-creation-realities music. Here is a song he wrote on the righteousness of God. I took the liberty to assign scriptural references to many of the lines to show the biblical basis for this music.

Many people in the Body of Christ fight unworthiness, shame, and condemnation. There is no shame or unworthiness in Christ, except when believers cling to a memory of sin. Singing songs like this aid believers in drawing nigh to God and resisting the devil. The song is entitled "I Am the Righteousness of God in Christ":[17]

- *I am the righteousness of God in Christ* (2 Cor. 5:21)
- *A brand-new creation in Him* (2 Cor. 5:17)

* *I can now approach the presence of God* (Heb. 4:16)
* *With no condemnation of sin* (Rom. 8:1)
* *I am the righteousness of God in Christ* (2 Cor. 5:21)
* *I am now complete in Him* (Col. 2:10)
* *I'm a partaker of His divine nature* (2 Pet. 1:4)
* *On me He will not impute sin.* (Rom. 4:8)

Much of the Church believes more in sin and the shortcomings of the flesh than in the in-Christ realities. I never moved out in the things of God while having a sin-conscious mentality. The devil's deception came even though I was born again and the righteousness of God in Christ (2 Cor. 5:21). You may have had the same experience.

What likely bothers you the most when God wants you to pray for someone sick or with another issue of life is a sense of unworthiness. The devil continually lies to you, trying to discredit God and His Word by reminding you of your unworthiness and what a dirty, old worm you are. These are all lies from the pit of hell! Our worth or sense of unworthiness has nothing to do with God's Word, except to rob you of your confidence. This lack of trust and certainty comes to stop your boldness, which is the very key to your success in prayer.

Preachers, religious people, and possibly parents and teachers—the authorities in your life—may have drilled this thinking into you. However, you cannot be saved, born again, a new creation in Christ, *and* still a sinner. These two persons cannot coexist. You are either saved *or* a sinner, but you cannot be both at the same time. In fact, there is nothing in those words *dirty, old worm,* or *unworthy* that agrees with God and His Word. Sin-consciousness—that is, a consciousness of your past and what you were before Christ—looms large in your mind, stopping you from stomping on the devil and receiving all that Jesus bought and paid for at Calvary. With a loser mentality, you become useless to God. I often say, "When God needs you the most, you are off having a pity party or dying somewhere."

The worship leader is a vital key, a tool of God, to build God-consciousness and faith in the congregation. We have already discussed the role of the worship leader in bringing people into a crescendo of faith and victory. A victorious, triumphant person in God is our status, and that is what we are to sing to thrust the Church into the presence of God.

In the Old Testament, God admonished the Jews to both speak and sing His Word. God told them to rehearse the words He gave to them and to keep those words before their eyes. The Lord told Joshua to meditate on the Word of

God both day and night in Joshua 1:8, and then he would prosper and have good success. Why? Joshua had a huge undertaking: to transport and deliver a million people to the Promised Land. That meant he had to know and to stay focused on God's Word. Meditating on the Word of God brings success and prosperity with it. Joshua needed this to successfully lead a million people into the Promised Land.

In Deuteronomy 31:19, God instructed Moses in a similar manner. He admonished Moses to rehearse and meditate the songs of the Lord as a way of training the people of Israel:

> *Now therefore write ye this song for you, and teach it to the children of Israel: put it in their mouths, that this song may be a witness for me against the children of Israel.*
>
> —Deuteronomy 31:19 KJV

If the people of Israel were to put the Law of God in their mouths, so are we. How do we put the song of the Lord into our mouths? We sing the Word. We speak the Word. We study and meditate on the Word. These activities put the Word of God in our mouths, our hearts, and our minds. Music makes it easier and more palatable to follow God's instructions. It is also an easier way to build the Word into our spirits.

Once we get the Word into our heart, speak it, sing it, and embrace the truth of God's Word, then it becomes ours. It will then be like Jesus' exhortation in John 7:38: "Out of [your] belly shall flow rivers of living water" (KJV). We feed ourselves with food for physical strength, and we must also feed our spirit man with spiritual manna to quicken and make us alive and become the life-giving force in the earth God planned and designed us to be.

The second verse of "I Am the Righteousness of God in Christ"[18] teaches us about the substitutionary work of Jesus Christ and the provision of our redemption in God:

- *He died to make us live* (1 Thess. 5:10)
- *To make us righteous He was made sin* (2 Cor. 5:21)
- *He became weak to make us strong* (Heb. 4:15; Eph. 6:10)
- *Suffered shame to give us glory* (Heb. 12:2)
- *He went to hell to take us to heaven* (2 Cor. 5:1)
- *Was condemned to justify us* (Rom. 8:1; 5:1)
- *He was made sick to make us well* (Gal. 3:13; 2 Cor. 5:21; Isa. 53:10)
- *Was cast out from the presence of God* (Ps. 51:11)
- *To make us welcome there.*

The Father God wanted a family, so He purchased us by Jesus' blood. He bought us back from Satan. Jesus broke the devil's authority over sin, sickness, and poverty once and for all by the blood of Jesus. He is the Lord of lords and the King of kings!

Through music, we build the anointing. The anointing is on the Word! So, sing the Word, and the anointing will automatically be there. When you do this, you charge the atmosphere, creating a place for Holy Ghost to manifest signs and wonders. By singing in-Him reality songs, we build an aura of faith through meditation on the Word.

It is also a great platform for singing psalms in a church service. People will be meditating (talking and singing to themselves) as they sing new-creation songs over and over. This should not take forty songs. It only takes about three songs filled with faith and victory and the name of Jesus. This is a powerful platform for your pastor to come right behind and preach.

As I've said before, in many charismatic churches, worship takes thirty or forty minutes, because people come to church with all the cares of this life on them. Most worship leaders push the people further down by singing songs that make them weep as they meditate and think about their hard lot in life. They sing songs filled with emotions, all about how they feel. This is not worship to

God. Soulish songs do not penetrate the throne room of God. Angels are just sitting on their hands waiting to hear God's Word so they can move in a congregation. You must discard the melancholy, emotional music if you want God to display His signs and wonders.

Let's consider other areas of ministry for which you need to prepare, such as healing lines and altar calls. During a healing line, you want to keep a good flow of faith coming into the believers' ears and hearts. Here is an example of a great song called the "Name of Jesus."[19] The chorus listed below is all about the power found in Jesus' name:

The name of Jesus is higher than all names
Just name a sickness, or any problem
At the mention of that name they bow, they fall
The name of Jesus is higher than them all.

You see, much of the Church world believes more in sin than they do in the power of the Word. To walk in victory, we must train and educate people into faith, so they will kick the darkness out of their consciousness. Sing the Word and let faith dominate their minds so it will affect their spirits.

You may have heard believers say, "I will probably die at fifty. That is when my daddy and my grandpa died. Cancer or heart disease runs in my family." No, no, a thousand times no! You must train and retrain people to believe the Word of God. They are no longer a son of whatever their family name is. They are sons of the living God! Cancer and heart disease do not run in the family of God! Change their doubt to belief by schooling them into faith through music.

Jesus conquered everything for us—sin, sickness, and poverty (Col. 2:15). Galatians 3:13 and 29 says that redemption from this threefold curse of the law is ours. Jesus' name represents all that He did at the cross. When they think about Jesus, what should they think about? Victory. Life. Eternal life. Satan's defeat. The blood of Jesus has cleansed them from all unrighteousness. They just have to name it.

Here is another great example of a faith song that declares the name of Jesus. It is entitled "He Is My Lord":[20]

Advocate, Anointed, Beloved, Bridegroom, Jesus
Captain, Covenant, Deliverer, Daystar, Jesus
Elect, Everlasting Friend, and Faithful Jesus
Governor, Gift of God, Hope, Head of the Church, Jesus.

I Am, Image of God, Judge, Just, Jesus
King of kings, King of glory, Light, Life, Jesus
Master, Messiah, Nail-Scarred, Nazarene, Omega,
Physician, Redeemer, Shepherd, Teacher, Unchanging Jesus
Very God, Word, Your Savior, Jesus.

Chorus:

I call Him Wonderful
I call Him Counselor
He is the Prince of Peace
He is my Lord
The King of Israel,
Jesus, Immanuel
Anointed, Living Word
He is my Lord.

I have sung this song thousands of times. Time after time, Holy Spirit has given me a word of knowledge for someone who was present in the room. The power of the name of Jesus brings all that His name represents to the circumstance. That name is healing; that name is deliverance; that name is redemption from sorrow and depression; that name is Jesus! When you sing the name of Jesus, you bring forth all that Jesus is to manifest in your very presence.

I am challenging you to change your music and worship and to school your people into faith. I have been across America and spoken in over a thousand Word churches. Yet I could count on one hand the number of churches who sing music declaring the Word of God or making faith proclamations through the music. Much of our church worship resembles the fragrance of God, but not the Spirit of Truth.

In fact, most congregations, and even most pastors, do not understand, nor do they preach redemption or new-covenant realities beyond salvation.

When Jesus died, and the veil ripped from top to bottom in the temple at Jerusalem, the Holy Spirit left the temple. The Jews retained their traditions. They did not even know the Holy Spirit had left. It sounds like the Word people. They have a great message of faith, but their worship is of the senses or the flesh, and they do not even know it.

Preachers have received the revelation of who they are in Christ and of faith and confidence in God. In the 1970s, they taught their people faith. If you teach people faith, then move on and teach people the next level of worship. Get into the New Covenant and into the new creation and move to the next level.

I have challenged you, but I am doing it in love. I know this is a challenge. Some people say this "David Ingles music" is hard. It is not hard. If I can play this music on the guitar, you can play it on the piano. It is not hard because you have an anointing from God (1 John 2:20), and you can do all things through Christ which strengthens you (Phil. 4:13).

God opened doors for me to sing the new-creation message and teach it across America. I have sung in the greatest places in the world. God rolled out the red carpet for me, and I would sing songs based on the epistles. Often, the congregations would not even understand the words of the songs, even in Word-filled churches. What a wonderful opportunity I had to minister some powerful truths. I had the greatest time there ever was on earth. This music is the greatest preaching outline in the world. It is such a great tool for ministry.

I used to be so tired from traveling that I wanted to be at home. Yet, when I sang the new-creation music, people would fall over under the power of God. This music has His anointing on it, friends. If you want to see people fall under the power of God, blind eyes see, deaf hear, and the lame walk, sing this music! I have seen miracle after miracle take place while I was singing the new-creation music.

I was once in Iowa by invitation of a Full Gospel Businessmen's Fellowship (FGBMI). Several people gave a testimony of their lives as sinners (before Christ). They shared the details of their life in sin. Personal testimonies are what draw people to these meetings. This organization in Iowa advertised my event. They even advertised miracles on large billboards.

Listen, signs and wonders follow the Word; they don't follow stories of troubles. I am not against people testifying about their troubles. Organizers of these meetings want to fill the house. They can bid them all to come if they want to talk about sinners' lives—but they should not expect miracles. If they sing those old soulish, emotional songs and tell testimonies of their lives before Christ, they will *not* get miracles. If they want somebody to get up and walk out of a wheelchair, they have to sing the Word!

In this Full Gospel Businessmen's meeting, an ex–drug addict got up and told jokes before it was my time to minister. And yet, they had a big poster of me on the wall, advertising the miracles that would happen that night. I thought to myself, *How are any miracles going to take place after this?* I went up to the stage and told everyone that if they wanted to leave, to go ahead and leave because no miracles would take place behind unbelief. I would have to sing the Word to get the Spirit of God stirred up, and then we would have some miracles. I said, "If you want to stay around, you are welcome to stay. If you want to leave, go ahead."

I started singing, and at about the middle of the third song, the gift of the word of knowledge started working. That is when the Holy Spirit reveals a piece of His knowledge, such as a sickness or disease that is present in the room. A little, emaciated woman who weighed about ninety pounds sat in the room, looking like skin and bones. She was just shaking. She fell out of her chair three times. Finally, I said, "God, if You do not tell me what to do here, she is going to fall out the fourth time."

God told me she had a blood disease. He said, *"If you just call her up here, I will heal her. When she comes up, she will be ringing wet with perspiration."* God did, I did, and she did. Her healing manifested instantly! Afterward, she looked like I had poured water over her.

Another young man, who had been injured in the Vietnam War, came up to the front; he had a steel plate in his head. He was bald with a paralyzed body, dragging his feet. I laid my hands on him, and he had a "glory hallelujah" instant miracle. It was so much fun!

And you know, all I did was sing new-creation music. I am not the healer. However, the anointing makes you bold as a lion. Jesus is the Healer! All I must do is talk about Jesus, lay hands on people, and He heals them!

The Word of God in music puts backbone in you. When you sing unbelief, you manifest or get unbelief. If you sing faith, faith manifests miracles. In Romans 10:17, the Bible says, "So then faith comes by hearing, and hearing by the word of God" (KJV).

There are no secrets in God. Holy Ghost unveils situations or things that are present to His men and women. The new-creation music taught me how to be sensitive to God. It made a new man out of this preacher. I would sit and sing the same song twenty-five or thirty times—just ministering to the Lord in my home. When we sing faith, when we sing about the name of Jesus, or when we sing victory in Christ and who we are in Him, it brings Holy Ghost on the scene. Angels will manifest signs and wonders as the Word of God comes out of our mouths in spoken word or music. Holy Ghost is the awesome power of God! He wants to show off and demonstrate Himself, bringing glory to Jesus Christ!

I have offered a challenge to you in this chapter about schooling your people in faith through music. Obviously, you are not going to dump all this on your congregation at one time, but you need to start somewhere in getting the Word of God into your people through music.

For every subject on which your pastor ministers, you should sing a song out of the epistles or backed by the Old Testament to accompany it. For example, when the pastor is to teach about Abraham, you ought to sing a song like "The Seed of Abraham":[21]

"Lift up your eyes and look
From the place where you now stand
North, south, east, and west
I'll give you all the land
To thy seed forever."
God promised Abraham,
"I will make thy faith seed
Number as the sand."

Chorus:

I'm of the seed of Abraham
And his blessings rest on me!
I'm of the seed of Abraham
I'm not moved by what I see;
Jesus was made a surety
And that's what I believe,
He's the seed of Abraham
And His seed remains in me!

Verse 2:
"I'll bless you going out
And bless you coming in.
Even the length and breadth
Of where your foot has been;
Fruitful I will make thee
And thy seed after thee,
In their generations
I'll bless exceedingly."

Here's the chorus of another song called "Abraham":[22]

Abraham, Abraham
Friend of God, Abraham
There was righteousness
Reckoned unto him
Father of nations, Abraham.

People say that their congregations cannot sing that, but I am not sure what they mean. People learn to sing, "Twinkle, Twinkle, Little Star." All you must do is start. Just buy the music, listen to it, and get it before their eyes. There is the eye gate, and there is the ear gate. This is how the spirit man hears and faith gets deposited in the heart.

When I traveled throughout the United States ministering in churches to raise money for missions, people would ask, "How do you use this music in talking about missions?" Listen, people do not want to hear about all the poverty in the world. All the money in America will not change the world. Jesus is the only thing that will change the world. I would minister Jesus and get the people so full of joy that they would get drunk in the Spirit. I have seen people get so happy that they would stand up to clap and then fall over under the power of God. One eighty-year-old woman crawled on the floor appearing drunk just like on the Day of Pentecost—all while singing this music. God will do it in your church, too. Initially, it may be a difficult thing. However, to move into a higher level of worship music, you will have to discipline yourself.

"You convinced me, Pastor Jerry, so how am I going to get this bunch out of their unbelief over into faith?" As the worship leader, you are on a mission or an assignment from God. Of course, you are going to use wisdom and a whole lot of love to convince your pastor of the power in this music. Sharing resources such as this book may be a good way to introduce him to the songs of the New Covenant Church.

God never did ordain you or me to split churches. God will exalt you if you submit to your pastor. Your job is to put your pastor over. You need to spend time alone with God to pray for him. How should you pray for him?

> *I . . . cease not to give thanks for you, making mention of you in my prayers . . . that . . . the eyes of your understanding [would be] enlightened. . . .*
>
> —Ephesians 1:16, 18

Brother Hagin once said that he prayed that prayer a couple hundred times by just leaving the scripture passage open in his Bible. He walked into his church and spent hours praying that prayer. He said that he did not know what happened, but after a while he was a teacher. Previously, he had been a fireball preacher. He started understanding the Bible better. After Brother Hagin received the power of this revelation, he began teaching Bible lessons in the afternoon. People in his church started coming in the middle of the afternoon to hear him teach. Men were taking off work to attend his afternoon Bible classes.

If you are a traveling minister, use the wisdom of God and the love of God to convince the pastor to sing this music. By ministering this music, God will exalt you as you submit to the pastor. You need to pray for the pastors to whom God sends you.

Brother Hagin tells of one church he pastored where he prayed the two prayers that the apostle Paul prayed in Ephesians 1 and 3.

> *Cease not to give thanks for you, making mention of you in my prayers; that the God of our Lord Jesus Christ, the Father of glory, may give unto you the spirit of wisdom and revelation in the knowledge of him: The eyes of your understanding being enlightened; that ye may know what is the hope of his calling, and what the riches of the glory of his inheritance in the saints, and what is the exceeding greatness of his power to us-ward who believe, according to the working of his mighty power, which he wrought in Christ, when he raised him from the dead, and set him at his own right hand in the heavenly places, far above all principality, and power, and might, and dominion, and every name that is named, not only in this world, but also in that which is to come: And hath put all things under his feet, and gave him to be the head over all things to the church, which is his body, the fulness of him that filleth all in all.*
>
> —EPHESIANS 1:16–23

> *For this cause I bow my knees unto the Father of our Lord Jesus Christ, of whom the whole family in heaven and earth is named, that he would grant you, according to the riches of his glory, to be strengthened with might by his Spirit in the inner man; that Christ may dwell in your hearts by faith; that ye, being rooted and grounded in love, may be able to comprehend with all saints what is the breadth, and length, and depth, and height; and to know the love of Christ, which passeth knowledge, that ye might be filled with all the fulness of God. Now unto him that is able to do exceeding abundantly above all that we ask or think, according to the power that worketh in us, unto him be glory in the church by Christ Jesus throughout all ages, world without end. Amen.*
>
> —EPHESIANS 3:14–21 KJV

By praying these prayers constantly over his congregation, his church changed. We refer to these prayers as the Ephesian prayers.

As a worship leader, it is up to you to upgrade your music. However, if your pastor is not in agreement, then you need to get into agreement with him. (We have already talked about the relationship between pastors and worship leaders.)

You must get the words of this music in front of the people. By placing faith-based music in front of your congregation's eyes and in their mouths, you are educating or schooling your people in faith. The Bible tells us that whatever is in the abundance of our hearts comes out of our mouths.

Remember, you cannot force anything down people's throats. We educate people into this music line upon line and precept upon precept. Perhaps you may introduce one of these "faith" songs by singing it as a music special. When you do, place the words of this song on the media or overhead projectors for the people to see. It is a combination of the eye gate, the ear gate, and the mouth that makes the biggest impact. As you sing the special, invite them to sing along with you. Later you may be able to add the song into your Sunday morning repertoire after introducing a song as a music special. My testimony of singing these songs was that, initially, my church thought I was prophesying.

These songs are powerful confessions to build your spirit, and they will change you and your church. You will reach a new level in God and in spiritual things.

Chapter Fourteen

Learning to Draw from Your Spirit

And the very God of peace sanctify you wholly; and I pray God your whole spirit and soul and body be preserved blameless unto the coming of our Lord Jesus Christ.

—1 THESSALONIANS 5:23 KJV

Do you realize, as I have mentioned already, that you are a spirit, you have a soul, and you live in a body? Your spirit does not sleep. When you wake up in the morning, sometimes a song is running around in you that stays with you all day. This is because your spirit was meditating on that song all night. And just as you opened your eyes, that song was there. It crept over into your mind. However, it came out of your spirit, not your mind. Faith comes out of your spirit. That is where faith works. It might be a song like "Our King of Kings":[23]

When life tries to crowd you with doubting
And reason is doubt in disguise
You hold the key to the kingdom
Sing out, and faith will arise.

Chorus:

Kings and priests He made us to be
We have what we say
We get what we see
Faith is the victory, and love is the key
Jesus is Lord and our King of kings.

Verse 2:

We wrestle not against flesh and blood
But principalities and powers up high
But the greater One is within me
And He's living big in me now.

These words will change your situation. Do you see the power of these words?

I say this because, after singing one of these songs, someone once stood up in the congregation totally healed! But I felt nothing as I sang it! I was in Hibbing, Minnesota, on the platform of a church, just singing my heart out. Suddenly, a girl fell out of her seat in the back of the room. A bloodcurdling scream emanated from her. I just stopped. I thought, *Boy, this is the worst crowd I have ever seen.* They weren't doing anything about it!

What I did not realize was that only I could hear the scream. It was a spiritual scream. She was choking on her tongue, but I heard a demonic scream come out of that young girl. By God's anointing on that music, I had stepped over into another realm. The congregation was still in the natural realm.

Somehow the anointing on that music brought deliverance to her. It stirred up that demon, who caused an epileptic seizure. She thrashed around on the back floor, and nobody even looked her way.

Finally, I set the guitar down and thought, *If no one is going to take care of this, then I will.* I walked to the back of the auditorium with everyone staring at me. By the time I got halfway to the back, they all knew what was going on. I went back to where she was and cast out the devil from her in the name of Jesus. I did not know that she had been doing that in this church previously. Later, they wrote me a letter explaining the situation.

This event happened while I was singing the names of Jesus in the song "He Is My Lord":[24]

Advocate, Anointed, Beloved, Bridegroom, Jesus
Captain, Covenant, Deliverer, Daystar, Jesus
Elect, Everlasting Friend, and Faithful Jesus
Governor, Gift of God, Hope, Head of the Church
Jesus.

Jesus totally delivered that young woman that day through this music. The healing in this seventeen-year-old girl was so effective that she later did a study on the names of Jesus, and she made it into a crossword puzzle. She sent it to me asking if I could use it. All of this happened by singing a song—the right song!

What you see in a move of God is the degree of clarity and purity of the Word of God you preach and sing. Now you must stir it up.

During the hardest times of my life, this music came out of my spirit because it was there in abundance. Songs of faith led me to victory during crisis moments of my life, such as car wrecks in which my children were involved and other opportunities of life to see my faith work.

On my first vocal CD, *Jerry Zirkle Sings,* I tell the story of one of my sons having a bicycle accident, going over a six-foot wall, and landing on his head. He had a huge baseball-sized knot on his head, which swelled his eye shut. At the same time, I was in my backyard instructing people about healing as they sat around a picnic table on a Sunday afternoon. After receiving the baptism of the Holy Ghost, I taught healing in my home. I would buy a big turkey and invite people who were sick to come. I would feed them both physically and spiritually.

On that day, I had a house full of people, when I heard a bloodcurdling scream coming down the street. You know the sound of your own child. I knew it was one of mine. I thought, *Boy, am I going to have to prove what I am teaching?*

As my son was coming around the corner, the Spirit of God spoke to me and said, *"Lay your hands on him and just speak peace."* As I did, he immediately stopped screaming. When I pulled his hands away from his face, I was devastated for a second as I saw the disfiguration on his head.

All the people were yelling, "Take him to the hospital! Take him to the hospital!" Trying to escape all the doubt and unbelief that was coming at us, I took my son into the house. My brother Jim, who was visiting from the mission field, was there. We went in and laid that boy on the sofa. These are things you do without thinking. I got two kitchen chairs. I sat on one with my guitar in hand, and I had my brother sit in the other chair. I said, "Jim, you put your hand on his head and pray in tongues." I looked up to the Lord and sang the chorus of a song called "I Will Praise Him in Everything":[25]

I will praise Him in everything
And thank Him for what He has done
I will fight the good fight till faith turns to sight
I'll run till the race is run.

That may sound crazy, but the peace of God filled me.

Isaiah 59:19 says, "When the enemy shall come in like a flood . . ." (KJV)—but I say, "When the enemy comes in, like a flood" God raises up a standard! Remember, man added the punctuation to the Bible. You must repunctuate it by putting a comma in the right place to signify God's character!

God flooded me with His presence in that moment. I said, "I am not standing for this. You are not going to have my son." I broke the devil's power and sang praises to God. I also sang, "Wonderful, Excellent, Mighty":[26]

Our Lord is wonderful in counsel
He's wonderful
Excellent in working
He's excellent
Mighty to deliver
He's mighty
Glory be to God forevermore!

And God healed my son! Right there in the middle of that crowd, God healed him! A great big, disfigured head became normal right in front of our eyes. My son got up and shook me away. I said, "Where are you going?" He said, "I'm going outside to go play." It was Sunday night. My son did not have any black eyes, bruises, or marks from the accident.

What caused that anointing to come up out of my spirit? It was already a part of my normal life, which included singing faith music daily. I was the total of my talking yesterday. It is a lifestyle of faith that brings results.

What is happening when you speak to something, and it does not move? Your faith is unstable. One day you are feeding yourself unbelief, and the next day you try to operate in faith. The following day, you put in unbelief. The day after that you say, "It is not always God's will to heal." Then you hear another preacher who says, "Yes, it is God's will to heal every time." And the next day you turn on the TV and the preacher says, "I do not care what you say. My mother was a good woman. She got all her children into the ministry, and she died with cancer. The reason we all got saved was because she got cancer." This practice of alternating faith and unbelief continually brings confusion to your spirit.

God did not give anybody cancer so He could win them to Christ. God does not use cancer, heart disease, diabetes, or any other disease to teach the Church. Cancer does not come from God in the first place. God put the fivefold ministry into the earth to mature the Church, yet people want to teach the Word of God by a person's example or experience.

You can use examples as windows into the Word, but you must use Scripture to teach the truth. Stand on the Word of God. If you do that, your spirit man will not be confused. When the enemy comes against you with pressure, then there will be no standard raised. "Jesus Christ the same yesterday, and to day, and for ever" (Heb. 13:8 KJV).

I have sung music all my life. I led worship, and I never missed a single service in my church in ten years. However, I never saw a miracle until I changed what I was singing. Charles Wesley's hymn "Oh, for a Thousand Tongues to Sing" is a great hymn. However, most church hymns have a couple of great verses and then a verse or two of unbelief. Charles Wesley, of course, filled with the Holy Ghost, wrote many great songs such as this one.

The apostle James tells us, "Let not that man think he shall receive any thing of the Lord. A double minded man is unstable in all his ways" (James 1:7–8 KJV).

All I am trying to say is to keep purity and clarity in the music. The hardest thing you must do in your church is to keep your music true to the Word of God. Music will cause the congregation to mature and develop in spiritual realities if you will sing faith-based or new creation–based music.

Chapter Fifteen

Traveling Ministry and Lessons Learned

Behold, I have set before thee an open door, and no man can shut it.

—REVELATION 3:8 KJV

MANY PEOPLE SHARE WITH ME THAT GOD HAS CALLED THEM into a preaching, teaching, or a music ministry, and they want to know how to start. The obvious answer is to read and study the Bible and get before God in prayer. Preparation is never lost time. You must also submit yourself under a pastor of a local church and become available to them in any position or place they ask you to serve. Wholehearted service without picking the task is imperative. This is step one. This is the beginning. Know that God directs each person differently, arranging open doors and connections prior to or after Bible training.

God supernaturally put me into the ministry after I prayed over a United States map in my home for several weeks. (Prayer is mandatory.) I had just completed my second year at Rhema Bible Training Center, and I had received multiple prophetic words about what God wanted to do through me. I shared earlier in this book how the Spirit of God spoke to me while I was on a mission trip to Guatemala. God told me He wanted me to minister as a psalmist as the first phase of my ministry, despite my complaint to Him that I wanted to be a teacher. He said the teaching ministry was for another day and a different phase of my ministry.

Nonetheless, I prepared for a traveling ministry. My wife was attending Bible school in the morning and my children were in school, so I gave myself to prayer during the morning time. As I was praying, the Lord reminded me how Brother Hagin had prayed, declaring that he would preach all over the state of Texas, and then he expanded to the Midwest, and eventually from coast to coast. I thought that if that approach was good for him, it was good for me, too.

I took a laminated map of the United States and placed it on my kitchen floor. I began to pray in tongues as I walked over the map, prophesying that I would preach from border to border and from coast to coast. I made declarations of where I would go and what I would do. I spent time in prayer at other times, as well. After praying for several weeks in this manner, I told the Lord I had prayed all I could about these open doors.

With five children, I usually had ten kids in the house when my children brought home all their friends. Added to the commotion and noise generated from a house full of people, the phone started ringing with calls from pastors I did not know. They were calling to invite me to meetings. While on the phone with a pastor one evening, the police chased a man through our front door and out the back door of our apartment. It was rather humorous later. Despite the noise and chaos in our apartment during these ministry invitations, God mightily showed up!

Before one evening was over, I had received seven phone calls from pastors around the United States asking me to come to their churches. I asked the Lord, "How do I know where I should go?" He told me to go where I had favor. So, I called them all back. Some of them said they would like me to come if I was ever in the area. Finally, one of the pastors said, "I will pay your airfare here and give you contacts of other pastors to help you minister in other meetings in the area." I decided that was the favor of God.

After graduating from Bible school, I was off to my first meeting. This turned into a traveling ministry of several years before God called me to pastor. I had prophesied these open doors in my prayer closet before the doors ever opened. God never does anything or brings anything into manifestation until He prophesies it. He is no respecter of persons. What He did for Brother Hagin, He then performed for me. As the Word says, "Jesus Christ [is] the same yesterday, and to day, and for ever" (Heb. 13:8 KJV). He will do the same for you.

It was in a time of prayer that God spoke to me and gave me my marching orders from Revelation 3:8: "Behold, I have set before thee an open door, and no man can shut it" (KJV). I *believed* this Word of the Lord that the Holy Spirit revealed to me. It became my favorite Scripture. I engraved it in wood and placed it in my office.

I share with people all over America who want to know how to start in the ministry. It is simple: Learn three chords on a guitar and five of David Ingles's songs, and that will take you around the world. This is what God did for me *and* through me. I boldly proclaim the truth found in the in-Him realities that changed my life such as redemptive realities, being the righteousness of God, and all the blessings and benefits that are ours as believers. These truths promote and cause believers to excel to the *more in God* that belongs to everyone.

I received a word from the Lord regarding the music I was to sing, which was who-we-are-in-Christ music. This music gives you something to say. This message transforms people who are sick of religion. It is past time the Church started singing the new-creation realities and started riding the high places with God. We are seated in the heavenly places in Christ Jesus. It is our position, according to Ephesians 1:3. Let's talk about it, sing it, and do it! Let's ascend and dominate on the earth while we are seated positionally in heavenly places.

Earlier we discussed the operation of the Body of Christ on the earth. Just as Jesus Christ submitted Himself to the will of the Father, we must submit ourselves to God. There is unity and harmony in the Godhead. To experience the manifest presence of God, the Spirit of God sets order and structure into His family and His Church. In the book of Ephesians, the apostle Paul discusses the alignment or protocol for this structure, including the Body of Christ, the local church, the family, and even between business owners and their employees.

As a traveling preacher ministering in another person's local church, I submitted to that local pastor. I was there by that pastor's invitation. I was not there to split that church, but to edify, to exhort, and to comfort. As a minister submitting in another pastor's church, I must locate where the church is doctrinally and pray about how I can edify them and bring them to another level.

I learned as a young person how to serve both my pastor in the local church and the traveling evangelist I assisted for many years. As part of the music team and/or choir, I learned how to hook up with my pastor. Traveling with an evangelist as a young man required me to prepare altar call songs to draw people to the altar. My advance planning included highlighting and selecting altar call songs from the hymn books. I could minister and sing salvation, commitment, and dedication songs at a moment's notice. I scoured the hymn books and learned songs on different topics so that the music flowed with the message preached. I learned early on that to experience continuity and consistency with a message, theme, or topic delivered by the minister mandated my preparation and readiness to move in song to harmonize with the message.

This is good counsel to worship leaders as valuable preparation for excellence of ministry. A further tip might be to recognize the songs and music your man or woman of

God prefers, to equip them to move with the Spirit. On one occasion when ministering with Dr. Kenneth Hagin, I knew to keep my songs to faith and the Holy Ghost as my place was to prepare the stage for him to move in the prophet's anointing and the supernatural.

It is vitally important to keep a united front so that the hearers recognize that all members of the ministry team are on the same page, flowing together to bring forth the goodness of the Lord. Maintaining a united front requires continuously speaking and communicating the same message from start to finish in the Word and in song. To do this, each person on the platform must adhere to and know the gift that is set before them.

Very early on as a young man, I learned to listen to the worship team or leadership preceding my ministry time, so I could gain an understanding of their beliefs and doctrine. A good rule of thumb is to locate a position of agreement, or common ground. This puts you on the same page with the people in the congregation. Assessing the doctrine of a church is key to knowing how to flow and minister to the people. When in new churches or with unfamiliar people, I listen to their music to locate where I can connect and engage in an area of agreement. Afterward, I can build, strengthen, and move them into a higher level with the Word of God.

In prayer, the Spirit of God told me that He would allow me to stand in the anointing of God if I declared and proclaimed my gift of psalmist before the congregation. He went on to say, *"You will never stand before an audience that I will not show you what they need."* When traveling on the road ministering as a psalmist, I tore up and threw away my sermon notes and simply flowed with the Holy Ghost. Twenty-five times a month for several years, God performed His *rhema* word through me. In every congregation where I ministered, God spoke to me about what the people needed. The rhema word I received years ago works today in ministry. Thank God for the Holy Ghost!

Standing before a congregation without notes or knowledge of what you are going to say or do can be very unnerving if you have never done it before. Many worship leaders and ministry gifts could not fathom this. I have had many young men who wanted to help me with worship. However, they had to be so super-prepared and know every song in advance. They would come undone and lose it when I said we had no list of songs. This upends musicians who normally have every song determined in advance. Preparation is necessary, but preparation for Spirit-led worship and ministry is by the Spirit. Trusting the Holy Ghost and hearing His voice and instruction is critical to supernatural ministry. Holy Spirit told me the psalmist ministry journey meant learning to hear God's voice and following it. Many ministers never enter this level of ministry due to discomfort and a need for control.

Professionalism is necessary and good, but it cannot take the place of the anointing and flowing with God. One must not discount the ministry of the teacher. Therefore, God gave us the fivefold ministry, and He tells us in I Corinthians that He gave a variety of operations and administrations to grow up the Body of Christ. However, in a psalmist ministry, you must minister to different spiritual needs at many different levels. It requires spontaneity and listening to the Holy Ghost.

I may have a general idea in my spirit where Holy Ghost might want to go. However, the Spirit of God may take me an entirely different direction. As a psalmist, I cannot prepare in my mind; it is a ministry out of the Spirit (from the Holy Spirit to my spirit). God may take me somewhere different than expected.

The Spirit of God knows the needs of the people. Once you are standing in front of a congregation, He could change everything. Many times, after strumming the first note on my guitar or hearing a worship song from the platform, in my spirit I would know what to do and I then follow His leading. This kind of ministry requires preparation in the Spirit. The anointing forces you to adhere to and clearly hear the voice of the Spirit of God so you do not fall flat on your face.

As I prepared to minister in churches, most of the time I did not know what God wanted to do. But time after time, someone in the congregation would stand up and prophesy. For example, on one occasion a woman prophesied before I was to take the service. She said, "I sent this man to you, and he will tell you of a land far away. He will tell you of My glory. He will tell you of My power. And the same things that he talks about, I will demonstrate in front of you."

After divine directions like that, it is clear what God wants to do. I would say to myself, *Oooh, that's good! Let's get this show on the road!* So, I would get up and talk about the dark land, the power of God, and the deliverance of God, and I would sing those songs that lined up with the Word that God had spoken by His Spirit. Whenever I followed the Spirit of God's leading, the power of God manifested in healing and deliverance in the people. God moved mightily!

Submission to Other Ministry Leaders

As I have already mentioned, many preachers today do not understand the concept of submission to other ministry gifts or to others in leadership. When you learn the art of serving others, more or greater doors open simply because you walked in humility and loved those you served. No ministry gift is exempt from the law of Christ to love and serve others. Even Jesus Christ Himself, while He was on the earth, submitted to the will of His Father (Matt. 20:28). The Trinity of the Father, Son, and Holy Spirit all submit one to another.

Men and women graduate from Bible schools without church or ministerial experience, and then they want to go pastor or preach. They may have head knowledge about the Word of God and ministry, but they are still spiritually unprepared. They have no experience in ministry. They are still novices. The apostle Paul told Timothy in 1 Timothy 3:6 not to put a novice into an office lest they fall to Satan's snare through pride.

There is more to the ministry than acquiring Bible knowledge and revelation of the Word. There is character development. There is excellence in ministry. There is ministerial experience. Most importantly, there are lessons learned in applying the Word of God. If a person is older and has served under other men and women of God before attending Bible school, much of this development may already be at their disposal. However, spiritual maturity and ministry experience do not come simply with age. Without this apprenticeship under a pastor, people easily quit, and they often become defeated and bitter. Or they simply fall into some deceptive trap of Satan.

We discussed the fivefold ministries and the ministry of helps earlier. Supportive ministries work in tandem with the fivefold offices. To learn how to minister in the forefront ministry or a fivefold office, there is an apprenticeship or training ground to the ministry. The ones who jump ahead often play into the devil's devices.

My counsel to young men and women coming out of Bible school who are called into the fivefold ministry is to find a pastor whom they can help. Be willing to do anything and everything your pastor asks. I often told my deacons and those involved in ministry of helps, promotion by God does not come by picking your job or position. Be willing to do anything your pastor needs in the local church. Growth comes through *doing* the Word (James 1:22). Promotion comes from God, not man (Ps. 75:6–7). God sees your faithfulness, and *He* exalts in due time (1 Pet. 5:6).

The Spirit of God once showed me that the mighty hand of God is the fivefold ministry in the earth—the apostle, prophet, evangelist, pastor, and teacher. Our faithfulness to God brings us before great men. Learning to humble ourselves and serve those whom God places around us is necessary for promotion. Some people never enter the ministry God has for them. This is primarily due to their obstinance and refusal to listen to the leading of God by submitting and committing to those under whom God places them. The entire chapter of 1 Peter 5 addresses this very subject.

Learn to submit to your pastor and all leadership in the local church. The apostle Paul told Timothy that God selects and positions those who qualify through faithfulness. God commits the ministry to faithful men and women. God's candidates for the fivefold ministry include people faithful in their church attendance who demonstrate excellence in performing their tasks without complaining, murmuring, and griping.

Chapter Sixteen

Miraculous Operations of the Holy Ghost in Ministry

And my speech and my preaching was not with enticing words of man's wisdom, but in demonstration of the Spirit and of power.

—1 CORINTHIANS 2:4 KJV

MY LIFE AND MINISTRY BECAME A DEMONSTRATION OF THE power of the Word of God. I have seen Holy Spirit perform

His Word over and over in my life. I have heard testimony after testimony of what God has done through the power of the name of Jesus. It is the name of Jesus taught in the early Church that produced miracles, signs, and wonders that turned the world upside down. Thank God He is still performing miracles today!

Here are a few testimonies of God moving mightily through His Word.

A man once came one thousand miles to join my church after he lost his job in his city. Somebody sent him some of my teaching tapes. He sold everything he had and moved a thousand miles to Broken Arrow, Oklahoma. In the first thirty miles, his car blew up. His trailer axle broke. He had to unload what he had. While traveling to Oklahoma, he stopped at a hotel and somebody vandalized his car, broke his window, and took all his belongings. All this happened while he was moving toward God. Satan came against the Word in him.

He arrived on a Sunday morning without his wife and son. I was sitting in my office on Monday morning, and the Lord started speaking to me about him. I thought, *How do I know all of this?* The Lord said that He was sending him to me, and he was obedient.

I made a few phone calls and found out he had rented a house. He had just enough money to get into the house. He was totally broke. He did not have one stick of furniture for the house. The only thing he owned was a lawn chair and one mattress. He had no refrigerator, no washer and dryer, and no sofa. He had lost it all.

I sat down and talked with him. As he started talking, he started pouring out his troubles. In the middle of his troubles, I said, "Let me stop you. You believe God sent you here? You believe I am to be your pastor?"

He said, "I know it. I know it, sir."

"Then we are going to start right now with me being your pastor. Tomorrow is going to be worse than today if you do not shut up. You are talking your problems. You have talked about them so long you've gone bankrupt."

God's anointing got all over me. I taught and sang faith music to him. I had him singing it, too. Getting the Word on a believer's lips releases faith. Within one month, he had a whole house full of furniture and a job. People in the church rallied around him and bought him furniture. My wife and I bought him a refrigerator and food to put in it. We had an old table but no chairs. I hired a man to bring the refrigerator to his house. I told him about his situation, and he gave him a washer and a dryer. Another family gave him a sofa and a chair. Overnight he changed his conversation, and the blessings of God started coming upon him and overtaking him.

A Miracle for My Youngest Son

My family of seven did not generally travel with me. Without a call of God, the traveling ministry scene gets old mighty fast. On one trip, my wife and five children decided to travel with me. We had arrived in a town, and the boys took their skateboards outside to play. Before dinner, I told them to jump in the tub. In the process of this, my youngest son, Dan, who is now a pastor, hit his eye on the faucet in the tub. I stood in front of my boy with blood pumping out of his eye.

Did you know your head will argue with everything that is in your heart? I was in more shock than he was. I tried to figure out where in the world I needed to put a tourniquet on his head.

Before this happened, however, through diligent study, I had put this music in my spirit over and over and over and over. My spirit man was full of God, so up out of me came the power of God, and out across my lips I spoke the creative power of God. The Spirit of God gave me a scripture to speak from Ezekiel 16:6 that stopped the flow of blood. The blood instantly ended, just like I had shut off a spigot on a water hose.

The wound looked like someone had taken a zipper and shut it. I sang a song. *Sing a song?!* I know it sounds crazy, but *there is power in praise!*

Where did I get the song I sang? When you minister twenty-five times a month playing your guitar and singing songs of faith, an atmosphere or aura builds around you until the devil cannot get in your head.

This is how you renew your mind and become transformed from the inside out. When your mind is filled with the Word of God through daily meditation and through putting the Word in your heart, you do not talk doubt. You do not listen to garbage. You just speak life. You start singing songs declaring the blessings of God that are yours in Christ. This builds a solid foundation of faith!

A Miraculous Occurrence in South Dakota

During one church service in the little town of Brookings, South Dakota, a young boy came up for prayer after service. It was a humdinger of a service, as they say. We had a Jericho march and everything. This boy acted a little crazy. I was tired when it was over, and I was sitting on the altar rail with my guitar. This little skinny boy came over and said, "Reverend Zirkle, do you have any anointing left?"

Now, you must know that anointing does not have anything to do with how you feel: "Faith is the substance of things hoped for, the evidence of things not seen" (Heb. 11:1 KJV).

I said, "I have lots of anointing."

He said, "Would you lay your hands on me? I want you to lay hands on me so I can have more anointing when I worship God." (This young man was the worship leader.)

When I laid my hands on him, he fell on the floor and started getting stiff, rigid, and kicking. For some reason, I thought he was putting on a show. I had never seen anyone do anything like that before. However, when he started turning green and purple, I realized that he was dying. I looked inside his mouth and saw he was swallowing his tongue. I did not know what to do. I had my guitar with me. I do not know why I did this, but I straddled him and sang a song called "There's Power in the Name."[27] The chorus goes like this:

There's power in the name, power in the name
Power in the name of Jesus.
Demons have to go because of what they know
They know there's power in the name of the Lord.

It may sound crazy, but he started recovering. I must have looked kind of funny straddling that young person. I was a fat butterball in those days, and he was a skinny boy. There I was, singing songs of deliverance over him. If you are going to work for God, you must leave your pride at home, along with your traditions.

God Shows Up in Oregon

I was in Oregon eating a steak one night when God gave me a word of knowledge in an unusual way. I thought my jaw had popped out of place. I could not enjoy the meal. It was the best piece of meat I had ever had, yet I could not chew it because my jaw hurt. Finally, I said to God, "It's not my jaw that has the problem. Okay, God, I hear You." My jaw then quit hurting, and I ate the meat.

When I got to the church, I did not feel a thing. But I said, "Who is the person who has pain in their jaw and cannot eat meat?" One man came forward. I prayed for him, "In the name of Jesus, be healed!" His jaw popped back in place.

God does not always speak to me like that, but He did that night. Sometimes we are just dull of hearing, so the Holy Spirit touches us in our physical body to get our attention. We see from this that God can speak to us and use the gifts of the Spirit in a variety of ways.

Once I said, "Who has something wrong with their teeth?" The impression was so light I almost missed it. It turned out that it was the gift of the word of knowledge. God never screams at you. He is a Gentleman. He is the most quiet, gentle voice inside of you.

El Shaddai Demonstrates Himself in Colorado

One time I was in Colorado Springs, Colorado. Holy Spirit said to me, "Do not talk about missions tonight. Just tell them how good a God I am."

"Oh, God! Is that what You want me to do?" I was not prepared in my thinking for that.

I was the speaker at a missions conference, but God said, "Do not talk about missions."

I thought, *Certainly, that cannot be from God. I am a speaker at a missions conference!*

But He said, "You talk about how good I am."

I obeyed God! I sang and talked about how good God was. I was just singing and laughing and having a good time. I got so full of joy, I fell over and bumped my guitar. As I was lying on the floor, I was thinking, *Lord, I hope I did not break my guitar. I am probably ruining this suit.* Those are not very spiritual thoughts.

Did you know you can fall under the power of the Spirit and still be conscious of everything that is going on around you? I was lying on the floor and thinking about my thirty-year-old guitar. It was worth a lot of money, and I liked that old guitar. I had bumped it when I fell.

I only owned one suit to my name, and it was gray. The floor was dirty. I was thinking, *I hope I did not break my guitar. They will think I am crazy for sure.* Then a lady stood over me and screamed out the loudest prophecy I had ever heard. What I did not know when I fell under the power of God was that everyone in the room had fallen under the power, too. I heard this crashing noise. I was in another realm, and I was not conscious of what was happening outside of my inner dialogue.

As I lay there, the Lord told me, *Because you told My people I love them, from this day forward, you will walk in a new anointing. Everywhere you go, this anointing will go with you because you told My people I love them. All your bills will be paid before they are due.*

They had a Jericho march while I was still lying there. I am telling you that your brain still works when you are slain in the Spirit. As I lay there under the anointing of God, with my brain roaming all over the place, I woke up under hundreds of twenty-dollar bills. The congregation had marched around me and covered me with money. I went there broke, and God showed Himself as El Shaddai, the God Who Is More Than Enough! Now, that is the way to take an offering and experience the blessing of God! Let God execute His plan, and superabundance comes to you.

You can laugh all you want. The crowd that night was probably under two hundred people, and they covered me with almost thirteen thousand dollars. Now, that is a miracle! Oh, the joy of the Lord is my strength!

Another Holy Ghost Happening in New Mexico

I am talking about the varied ways Holy Ghost moves. A man in New Mexico once told me, "I cannot believe a man has a ghost living in him." I was about ready to miss an airplane, and he was angry. A doctor had surgically removed his vocal cords, and he had a microphone connected to his throat to talk. My compassion at this point had flown out the window. I had driven a hundred miles out of my way to pray for him, and he stood there telling me off. My patience was severely waning. I was ready to tell *him off.*

I kept looking at my watch. I thought, *If I break every speed limit in New Mexico, I still might not catch my airplane.*

Finally, I thought, *I do not have enough time to teach him all about healing.* I said, "Why don't you let me pray for you using my own faith?"

God healed him that day! He was a college professor and a very quiet man. His head had gotten in the way of him receiving from God. After he was healed, his wife said that he carried our prayer letters in his pocket, and he read them in his bedroom.

God meets people right where they are. We all need Jesus Christ. We all need to be baptized with the Holy Ghost, overflowing with the language of love. By receiving the Holy Ghost, people quit having blue Mondays. He fills in the valleys, levels out the mountains, and straightens out the crooked places. Holy Ghost gives believers the power of God to live victoriously. The baptism in the Holy Ghost happens just like the new birth: by faith!

Many people are afraid of the baptism with the Holy Ghost because they have heard so many crazy stories. The Holy Ghost baptism is the greatest and best thing that ever happened to me. Everything with God is simple. Too often, preachers complicate the things of God. We receive the Holy Ghost the same way we receive every other God-given benefit—by faith!

We are in the book of Acts extended! Jesus has not come for His bride yet. Until then, we must occupy till He comes. When people say the apostles died out with the first church, then you and I must have missed the rapture. Believe me, I did not miss the rapture. I am still here. It is still the first church! We have been writing chapters since the first century! The twenty-first century is no different.

There are more chapters to be written by Spirit-filled fanatics like you and me.

Chapter Seventeen

Becoming a Force for the Kingdom of God—Transition from Bible School to Ministry: Where Do I Start?

God used me throughout my years of ministry in all the fivefold areas of ministry, and yet I am a pastor at heart. Over the years, I have pastored hundreds of people who wanted to do something for God in full-time ministry. I have heard testimony after testimony coming from ministers who shared the same thought. They said that they learned the Word of faith by attending a Bible school, but they learned how to apply the Word of faith under our pastorate. What are they saying? They learned the Word of God, but they did not know how to apply the Word in situations that required it, either in personal or ministry life.

It is my belief that many people attend Bible schools founded and directed by evangelists, and that these students need to sit under a pastoral gift to prepare for the fivefold ministry, especially the pastorate. In 1 Timothy 3:13, Paul told Timothy deacons should "purchase to themselves a good degree, and great boldness in the faith" (KJV). I touched earlier on the fact that there is an internship to the ministry.

Many people wreck their lives and the lives of their congregations by not training under a pastoral gift. Oftentimes, these young leaders become discouraged, bitter, and hopeless. Some even fall away from God and the Church altogether.

I told my deacons who went out to start churches, that if they got out there and had a negative church experience, they needed to come back and be a deacon a bit longer. I did not want them to take any more laps around the mountain. An internship in the ministry equips a minister to override many hindrances and roadblocks Satan erects to stop them from fulfilling their calling and finishing the course God ordained. Too many times people jump out too soon, thinking they got it. They just needed a little more refining and grooming.

If a person completes Bible school and wants to know what the next step is, here is my pastoral counsel: Go find a good pastor that you can help and be their right-hand person so you can learn the trade directly from a man of God. Just like any skilled job, you do not start right off as a carpenter. You must become a journeyman first. There are steps involved to reach the top. This is true in ministry as well. As a deacon, you purchase to yourself a good degree. This is preparation for the ministry. You learn the frailty of men and woman who are born again but still housed in flesh, and you learn how and if you can help them. This is invaluable knowledge!

Stay in faith, expectation, and the love of God. Above all, *do not quit*. By doing this, you become a candidate for the fivefold ministry. Be willing to teach in the children's church or work behind the scenes when no one is looking and applauding you. Ministry—and especially pastoring—is 10 percent forefront and 90 percent behind the scenes.

Your job as someone helping your pastor is oftentimes to do the dirty work, the manual labor, like the first deacons did in the early Church. They were not preaching. They were keeping all the widows from getting in catfights and keeping everyone happy by the Holy Ghost. Can you do that? If not, you are not ready yet for the ministry.

As we shared, an apprentice lifts the hands of their pastor. As I mentioned before, do not pick your job. Be willing to do anything they ask you to do and do it under their guidance and direction. Become so invaluable to that pastor that they must chase you down the road promoting you into your own ministry or put you on the payroll. This is as soon as you are ready for full-time ministry. If you can do anything else and be satisfied, you are not ready for the ministry.

There is a wide door of opportunity for ministry all over the world. Hundreds of pastors drop out of the ministry every year because they did not fine-tune their skills and help a man of God long enough to mature in character and integrity. The sooner you submit to the internship, the sooner God can thrust you forth to be a force for the Kingdom of God. It's like the song "This Is Our Finest Hour"[28] says:

Chorus:

This is our finest hour
For every field is white
And the Spirit of the living God is on us
To bind up broken hearts
To cause the blind to see
This is our finest hour
to set them free.

Verse 1:

Let's not be discouraged by the enemies of life
Thoughts that try to tell us we can't win
Let's remember God is able
And willing to perform His Word from the beginning to the end.

Verse 2:

Harvest now is ready, and workers are so few
And there are those who yet have never heard
Let's just keep on doing
What God tells us to do
Living in and giving out His Word.

God has ordained every believer from the foundation of the earth to be useful in the Body of Christ. Many refuse to grow and develop into stalwart believers to impact the community and world to which God calls them. If you have reached this chapter, you are one of those who are ready and willing to eat the good of the land and to be used in this last-hour army of God.

Remember, God has a place for *you* at the table of provision. He equipped you from the foundation of the earth to fulfill your calling. He is unwilling to do without soldiers in His army. You can remain a corporal, or you can ascend to become a general by the development of your spirit, the renewal of your mind, and the discipline of your body to the Word of God. I encourage you to experience all that God has for you by meditating and singing the Word of God and fulfilling the great plan that God has designed for you.

My vision for our church was simple: Sit down, shut up, and grow up. It starts with sitting down under a pastor, shutting up (listening to the Word of counsel from a spiritual parent), and growing up (becoming a useful member of the Body of Christ)!

Chapter Eighteen

Final Thoughts for Living Victoriously in Christ

WE SERVE A GOD OF MIRACLES! HE IS READY TO MOVE IN the lives of believers today, just like He did in the early Church. We discussed throughout this book miraculous happenings that occurred through people speaking and singing God's Word. The open door to the supernatural is the spoken Word of God—the *rhema* of God. Everyone wants to see a spectacular move of God. However, to operate in signs and wonders, a hungry heart for God is an essential ingredient. To be used of God in the miraculous, we must want it for the right reasons.

Walking with God in ministry is truly a journey, not a destination. The Christ-life is fluid, changing, and always transformative. The Father never dictates your life. He offers a choice: Either live for Him, with Him, and unto Him, or follow the route of the flesh (led by the adversary) to sin, disobedience, and failure.

Every day you and I choose life or death, blessing or cursing. God tells us in Deuteronomy 30:19 to *choose life!* Who does not want life and blessing? We must, on purpose, choose God in order to experience God's best. He promised humankind a long, strong life (Gen. 6:3), but many people choose to quit somewhere along the way.

We understand it is the diligent who make their way prosperous and successful; the fool comes to ruin and destruction (Prov. 12:24; 21:5; Josh. 1:8). Many people choose to quit; give up; decide it is too hard, difficult, or impossible; and lie down.

These were never choices I chose along the way, though many people challenged me to do just that. People want you to join with them in their same mediocrity, conformity to the world, and misery. Admittedly, my earthly dad, my spiritual mentors, and my heavenly Father never offered those as options to me. My early foundation in Christ created a picture of promise, hope, and fulfillment.

A primary lesson I want you to take away from this book is the value and mandate to live your life in the Spirit. Only a life lived from the reborn human spirit produces a victorious and abundant life in Christ. We discussed how God is a Spirit and His fellowship with man is through the re-created spirit. To know God is to commune with Him in the Spirit.

We know that faith pleases God (Heb. 11:6). Learning or choosing to yield to God in every moment, segment, and decision is the choice we must make to follow where God leads. It must become a lifestyle or habit—one in which we do not depart. The path of least resistance usually is not of God; it is the devil's way to distract us and keep us in a life of comfort and ease. God never called us to a life of ease.

I have challenged people all over the world with this nugget of truth: "Pressure either molds you into the image of God or moves you down the road where you are comfortable." Choosing Christ and His Word puts you on the edge of disaster or on a narrow precipice. Only active, creative faith can deliver you. Our journey with Christ is a series of choices. The key to following God's plan is praying in the Spirit, yielding to His voice, and then obeying it when no one else agrees. Courage is not the absence of fear but fulfilling the call in the midst of formidable obstacles and seeming impossibilities.

Over the years, great opportunities to travel and minister with great men of God have opened to me. The opportunity for greater influence and approval of men was available. If I told you the names of these spiritual giants, you would know them. Listen, your character is the highest priority to becoming a success with God, and even man. Oftentimes, the non-glamorous people in God's plan make the greatest impact.

I learned a valuable lesson from Brother Hagin: "The inward witness is just as supernatural as guidance through visions...it is just not as spectacular. Many people are looking for the spectacular and missing the supernatural that is right there all the time."[29]

Jesus was led by His re-created spirit into the wilderness to be tested by Satan for forty days and nights. The apostle Paul spent years in isolation, separate from the acclaim and praise of the apostles or the Church-at-large. And Moses, the great champion of God, spent years in seclusion, learning to walk with God without acclaim and notice. These are not popular ideas that believers want to hear, yet it is in the hard places that most spiritual growth occurs.

Finding and following God's path is learning the way of the Spirit. Throughout this book, we talked much about the Holy Ghost and learning to be sensitive to Him. Worship is both spirit and truth. So much of the time, people follow the crowd and entirely miss God's anointing and flow in their lives and ministry. However, by following the still, small voice or adhering to the green light inside of our spirits, Holy Ghost keeps us out of a lot of ditches, misfortunes, and regrets. Thank God for Holy Ghost, who always leads us into triumph and His perfect will!

Here are some other nuggets of truth for consideration to empower you to stay on *your* path and fulfill the plan of God for *your* life. These are a few of the principles addressed in this book. Each concept counsels us with a vital key to winning in life and becoming the mature sons and daughters of God the Holy Spirit desires us to be.

- Read the Bible daily!
- Meditate, think on, and chew on God's Word throughout the day.
- Stay built up and edified in the Word through singing the Word of God!
- Worship and pray in tongues continually. Praying in tongues makes you irresistible!

* Be available to God twenty-four hours a day, seven days a week! Many people miss God's plan because they are not available when God needs them. It usually is not convenient when He calls you to an assignment.
* God does not need your ability; He is looking for your availability. It is your availability to God that opens greater doors of opportunity. God once told me, "Son, the greatest door of ministry is the very one that I open for you."
* Always be ready to dump your plan for God's plan in a New York minute.
* Never stop learning, reading, and growing.
* Be teachable—do not be a know-it-all.
* Be pliable in the hands of the Holy Ghost.
* Be ready to do whatever Holy Ghost asks you to do right then and there—no questions asked! Many miracles or lives are shortchanged of God's power because the ministry gift was not instant in season and out.
* Always submit to those whom God has put in authority over you. Prefer and love everyone. Fivefold ministers are not exempt from practicing this biblical guidance.

* Forgive instantly and never take offense. The greatest enemy to a move of God or hinderance to the blessing of God is strife and offense.
* As with any gift, there are levels of development and anointing, so the more you yield to God in ministry, the greater and more profound the gift will be.
* Remember, God does not want us taking shortcuts and being manipulative. Faith can get us everything we need, but it requires effort and doing things opposite of the world's system and our senses. Pursue the way of faith in God's Word, and you will always win!

Notes

Endnotes

1 Kenneth E. Hagin, *Authority of the Believer* (Tulsa, OK: Faith Library Publications, www.rhema.org, 1975).

2 Kenneth E. Hagin, *New Thresholds of Faith* (Tulsa, OK: Faith Library Publications, www.rhema.org, 1986).

3 David Ingles, second verse of "You are Free," *Garment of Praise: The Songs of David Ingles* (Tulsa, OK: David Ingles Music, 1997), 42.

4 David Ingles, "Garment of Praise," *Garment of Praise: The Songs of David Ingles* (Tulsa, OK: David Ingles Music, 1997), 31.

5 David Ingles, "Our King of Kings," *Garment of Praise: The Songs of David Ingles* (Tulsa, OK: David Ingles Music, 1997), 12.

6 David Ingles, second verse of "Satan Has Been Paralyzed," *Garment of Praise: The Songs of David Ingles* (Tulsa, OK: David Ingles Music, 1997), 17.

7 David Ingles, "The Song of the Lord," *Garment of Praise: The Songs of David Ingles* (Tulsa, OK: David Ingles Music, 1997), 25.

8 David Ingles, "I Don't Sing Those Songs Anymore," *Garment of Praise: The Songs of David Ingles* (Tulsa, OK: David Ingles Music, 1997), 14.

9 David Ingles, "(Go Back) She's Using That Name," *Garment of Praise: The Songs of David Ingles* (Tulsa, OK: David Ingles Music, 1997), 57.

10 David Ingles, "Living in the Presence of Jesus," *Garment of Praise: The Songs of David Ingles* (Tulsa, OK: David Ingles Music, 1997), 41.

11 David Ingles, "That's What I Have, That's Who I Am," *Garment of Praise: The Songs of David Ingles* (Tulsa, OK: David Ingles Music, 1997), 18.

12 David Ingles, "Our King of Kings," *Garment of Praise: The Songs of David Ingles* (Tulsa, OK: David Ingles Music, 1997), 12.

13 Kenneth E. Hagin, *Tongues: Beyond the Upper Room* (Tulsa, OK: Faith Library Publications, www.rhema.org, 2007).

14 David Ingles, "In the Chamber," *Garment of Praise: The Songs of David Ingles* (Tulsa, OK: David Ingles Music, 1997), 2.

15 David Ingles, "El Shaddai (You're Such a Good God to Me)," *Garment of Praise: The Songs of David Ingles* (Tulsa, OK: David Ingles Music, 1997), 62.

16 Alliene G. Vale, "The Joy of the Lord" (His Eye Music, 1971).

17 David Ingles, "I Am the Righteousness of God (in Christ)," *Garment of Praise: The Songs of David Ingles* (Tulsa, OK: David Ingles Music, 1997), 2.

18 David Ingles, "I Am the Righteousness of God (in Christ)," *Garment of Praise: The Songs of David Ingles* (Tulsa, OK: David Ingles Music, 1997), 2.

19 David Ingles, "The Name of Jesus," *Garment of Praise: The Songs of David Ingles* (Tulsa, OK: David Ingles Music, 1997), 48.

20 David Ingles, "He Is My Lord," *Garment of Praise: The Songs of David Ingles* (Tulsa, OK: David Ingles Music, 1997), 59.

21 David Ingles, "The Seed of Abraham," *Garment of Praise: The Songs of David Ingles* (Tulsa, OK: David Ingles Music, 1997), 13.

22 David Ingles, "Abraham," *Garment of Praise: The Songs of David Ingles* (Tulsa, OK: David Ingles Music, 1997), 74.

23 David Ingles, "Our King of Kings," *Garment of Praise: The Songs of David Ingles* (Tulsa, OK: David Ingles Music, 1997), 12.

24 David Ingles, "He Is My Lord," *Garment of Praise: The Songs of David Ingles* (Tulsa, OK: David Ingles Music, 1997), 59.

25 David Ingles, "I Will Praise Him in Everything," *Garment of Praise: The Songs of David Ingles* (Tulsa, OK: David Ingles Music, 1997), 26.

26 David Ingles, "Wonderful, Excellent, Mighty," *Garment of Praise: The Songs of David Ingles* (Tulsa, OK: David Ingles Music, 1997), 21.

27 David Ingles, "There's Power in the Name," *Garment of Praise: The Songs of David Ingles* (Tulsa, OK: David Ingles Music, 1997), 60.

28 David Ingles, "This Is Our Finest Hour," *Garment of Praise: The Songs of David Ingles* (Tulsa, OK: David Ingles Music, 1984), 70–72.

29 Kenneth E. Hagin, *"How You Can Be Led by the Spirit of God"* (Tulsa, OK: Faith Library Publications, www.rhema.org, 1989), 34.

Jerry Zirkle

Pastor – Teacher – Psalmist

Jerry is best known for his familiar voice on the Oasis Network, Tulsa, Oklahoma, spanning 35 years, where he began broadcasting in 1986. Ministering as a psalmist throughout the U.S. and overseas, he has seen the lame walk, the blind see, and many other miracles through singing New Creation music.

Born in Akron, Ohio, he began his singing ministry as a young boy. He and his brother Bob ministered for over 30 years on the radio and in churches in a 10-state area. Once baptized in the Holy Ghost, his changed life led him to receive further Bible training at Rhema Bible Training University. In 1980, after graduating from Rhema, he and his brother Jim were ordained from their home church in Ohio, Living Water Fellowship. In the same year, they co-founded Living Water Teaching, a mission organization to reach Central America. Jerry spent the next three years preaching the uncompromised Word of God and singing scripture-based music of David Ingles and promoting Living Water Teaching.

In 1982, Holy Spirit led Jerry to start Living Water Teaching Church as a spiritual covering and location to train new missionaries coming to work on the mission field. In 1990,

Lester Sumrall ordained Jerry through the Lester Sumrall Evangelical Association. Over the next 12 years, Living Water Teaching Church and its missions outreach in Broken Arrow, Oklahoma, grew to over 400 church members and 100 missionaries in Central and South America, Japan, Germany, and Africa. Under Jerry's direction, this local church provided a base for training men and women to build the Kingdom of God at home and abroad.

In 1994, Jerry resigned from Living Water Teaching, at the Lord's instruction. He began traveling the United States and Canada, ministering the uncompromised Word of Faith in music and the spoken Word. In January 2000, Jerry Zirkle began Our Finest Hour Church in Broken Arrow, Oklahoma. As a pastor-teacher, Jerry preaches God's Word clearly and boldly, setting a high standard of excellence in spiritual and practical applications.